CW01551206

A Silly Girl with a Silly Hat

Deb Cooper

Published by New Generation Publishing in 2021

Copyright © Deb Cooper 2021

First Edition

The author asserts the moral right under the Copyright, Designs and Patents Act 1988 to be identified as the author of this work.

All Rights reserved. No part of this publication may be reproduced, stored in a retrieval system or transmitted, in any form or by any means without the prior consent of the author, nor be otherwise circulated in any form of binding or cover other than that which it is published and without a similar condition being imposed on the subsequent purchaser.

ISBN
    Paperback   978-1-80031-513-6
    Hardback   978-1-80031-512-9

www.newgeneration-publishing.com

 New Generation Publishing

In Deb's original manuscript there were blank spaces, and notes that Deb had made. She was planning on returning to these, to edit and complete the gaps in the narrative. Deb passed away before she was able to do this.

So, where there were gaps, the missing pieces have been filled in, to help the account flow and to expound on any notes that Deb had made.

Some names have been changed to protect people's identities.

Deb wrote the title *A Silly Girl with a Silly Hat* to add a lighter note to her story. It is in reference to a fluffy hat Deb used to wear to keep warm after she lost all her hair whilst having chemo. Deb was never to be seen in bed without this hat and as she would often say, "you get quite cold with no hair, you know!" Although Deb's 'silly hat' isn't mentioned in Deb's story, it is the family's desire to honour her wish and use the title she wrote.

All proceeds will go to charities and people in need.

It is the family's wish that this book points only to the Lord Jesus. They do not want any sympathy or to be put on a pedestal, but that their Saviour might be glorified. Many families go through difficult times and they are all unique and hard. Deb felt that she should share her story, so that it might be of help to others. We are commanded so many times in God's Word to speak of what the Lord has done for us and it can be put in no better words than the psalmist writes.

'Come and hear, all ye that fear God, and I will declare what he hath done for my soul.'
Psalm 66:16

To Mum, Dad, Tom and Becca and Steve – I'm sorry for everything I put you through. Thank you for forgiving me.

To Mash – The love of my life – Thank you for loving me – warts and all.

Forward

This is Deb's story, written in Deb's own words. It is a story of God's great grace and love towards 'just a silly girl', as Deb would call herself.

Deb was very dear to me, she was my sister, the girl who I grew up with. We shared a bedroom for eighteen years, we bickered and argued, we held 'mothers' meetings late into the night. Deb was also my best friend. I remember after our son Daniel passed away, she came and stayed with us and she just quietly sat, her presence being a great comfort, without the need for words.

When Deb was told that she was terminally ill, she said to me that she didn't know the future but that she felt strongly that she should write her story down.

Before Deb passed away, she asked if I would write the forward to her book. We as a family have walked this path together and, in a way, Deb's story is a part of us all.

Towards the end of Deb's life, when she began to get very poorly, I was having another sleepless night and had a feeling of such despair, the realisation was beginning to sink in, that Deb was soon to be going home to glory. The feeling of grief was overwhelming, and I was tossing and turning. I picked up one of Spurgeon's daily reading books, the text for that day was:

'But the dove found no rest for the sole of her foot, and she returned unto him into the ark, for the waters were on the face of the whole earth: then he put forth his hand, and took her, and pulled her in unto him into the ark.'
Genesis 8:9

In the dark of the night that verse became so dear to me; it was one of those precious moments when you hear the still small voice of the Lord speaking. This verse summed up to me Deb's life and story. Deb had returned unto the Lord and it was His kind hand that brought her back and was now drawing Deb in unto Himself into the ark. Her work and suffering on this earth were coming to an end, and the Lord was calling Deb to her eternal home.

So, as you read this raw and honest story, think on the love and forgiveness of a wonderful Saviour. A love that is so undeserved by us all and forgiveness that is so great and free.

One

10th September 2014

Tap, tap, tap, went Mash's foot on the dull grey tiled floor, his knee bouncing in time to the sound. Letting out a deep sigh he turns to look at Deb sitting next to him and rested his forearms on his thighs for what felt like the hundredth time. The curly haired brunette nervously spins round as she hears a door open and a name called. A sigh escapes her lips as she returns his gaze. The pain in her eyes matches his. When will her name be called? The wait felt like hours but in reality, had been closer to one. Further along the row of orange padded hospital chairs, sits her mum, Mary, her hands clutching her handbag desperately trying to keep a conversation going with her other daughter, Becca. Anything to distract from the intensity of the moment. Risking another look towards the consulting room doors, Deb's eye catches that of a heavily pregnant lady who lays one hand protectively on her extended abdomen.

'This is cruel.'

Mash's knee stops bouncing and he wanders towards glass doors overlooking a garden. Turning to look at her daughter, Mary offers up a quick prayer and makes a comment about the flowers in the garden.

"Deborah Dawson," calls the nurse, scanning the waiting room with expectant eyes.

Relieved the wait is over, Deb jumps up. She hesitantly steps towards the nurse, on legs of lead. A strong hand presses the small of her back, a silent message of reassurance and love. She must keep walking and blindly she follows the nurse, all senses numbed, barely hearing or acknowledging anything said.

A door is open ahead and in they go. A bare room, chairs around the edge filled with people, people smiling. Is that uncertainty in their eyes? Two chairs are vacant in front of a desk. A familiar face, Mr Townsend.

"Nice to meet you," she hears a voice say.

Did she just introduce Mash as her fiancé? The word sounded new and unfamiliar, and for a moment Deb was filled with love as she watched her future husband sit down his gaze meeting hers. Uncertainty showed in his eyes and Deb knew he was being strong for her. He, her strong and dependable one. What a precious gift God had given her.

"Do you mind all these people being in here?" Mr. Townsend said, bringing her back to the present. Cautiously turning to eye up the people on the chairs, 'What were they all doing and why so many?' Deb wondered as they each offered a smile while being introduced.

"No, it's fine," said an abrupt voice.

'I must sound so rude,' thought Deb, just wanting Mr. Townsend to finish with the formalities and just say what he had to. Today was the day of answers. Today they were going to find out what was going to happen next. This moment shaped the rest of their lives.

Two

I studied my reflection in the mirror. I liked what I saw. The skirt was short and showed off my long legs, especially with the help of the black heels. A moment of guilt passed through my mind. The top was low. Lower than anything I'd worn before. 'What would Mum and Dad say if they could see me now?' They knew I was staying at Tina's house but they didn't know what we were going to do.

"Are you ready?" called Tina from the hall.

With one final glance at the long mirror I spun round, grabbed my bag and headed for the door. Tonight, is just a one-off, I'm going to make the most of it, besides I'm eighteen now. I'm entitled to have some fun. Nobody needed to know. Besides, tomorrow morning I will be sat in chapel like nothing had happened.

"Coming," I replied, all traces of guilt were removed and replaced with a sense of excitement and adventure.

The singing sounded loud and the organ seemed to send vibrations through one's body, adding to the pounding headache. Finally, the hymn ended and I sank wearily down onto the pew. It didn't matter that they were uncomfortable. It was lovely to rest my sore feet. The minister opened his Bible and announced his text. My mind drifted to the night before. The club was smaller than I thought, and it had been so hot. I could almost hear the repetitive beat of the music and see the mass of bodies all moving in time. The drinks had tasted good and I had enjoyed the feeling of freedom and confidence they had given me. It was nice to be admired and to receive the attentions of a man, even if he seemed to enjoy my skirt rather than my smile.

Ouch! My head dropped back, cricking my neck. Panic caused me to grab the Bible, halting its descent off my lap towards the floor. The awful realisation that my eyes had been shut hit and I tried to focus on the minister's face wondering why I felt so nauseous. Risking a side long glance, I saw that Mum was looking at the minister too. 'Phew that was close'. This was going to be a long service.

November 2007

My phone vibrated against my leg. This time I knew I had to look at it. There was no way I could ignore it again. Excusing myself from the room, I found the bathroom and put my hand in my pocket. It was nice to spend time with friends from church and the lunch had been lovely. It seemed such a shame I couldn't relax like I used to. Why couldn't he just leave me alone just for a few hours? 'Just tell him,' said a voice in my head. I can't tell him now, it's too late, anyway he wouldn't understand. Things had gone too far. I wished I had told my parents about Fred before things had gotten out of hand, but the right time never seemed to come. I wished I had told Fred who I really was and that I spent each Sunday with my family going to church.

Deb, what are you up to? Why aren't you replying? I want to see you. Something's not right. Have I upset you?"

The text sent alarm bells ringing in my head. He didn't trust me, but then why should he? Why so insecure? Could I trust him? I thought back to the night before. "I love you, Deb, and will do anything for you. We are similar, you and me. Nobody understands us but we understand each other. It's a sign we are made for each other. I will always love you, nothing will ever hurt you because I won't let it." He ran his hand possessively down my back and I knew what he was thinking of next.

"I'm just round my parents' friend's house. Sorry I didn't reply, left my phone in my bag. Can't come around tonight am tired but will come and see you before work. What u up to?"

More lies. Lies that need backing up with more lies. The

truth felt so far away. It's tiring trying to maintain a double life. 'Begin again and tell the truth,' came the voice again.

Replacing my phone back into my pocket I headed back to the lounge. The subject had changed and the conversation had turned to the minister that day. It seemed everybody liked him and found plenty to agree with him about. My mind switched off. How boring. I couldn't even remember what he'd said. Maybe getting away from this life wouldn't be so bad after all. Besides looking around now nobody looked as if they would miss me.

April 2008

"I've missed you," said Fred as he wrapped his arms around my slight body. I leant into him, enjoying the feeling of being wanted.

"You saw me Friday."

"Yes, but I want to see you every day. I don't like it when I don't know what you're doing. It makes me think you don't want to be with me any more. Maybe you're seeing someone else."

"As if I would! You know I'm yours. You know me better than that."

"Yes, you are mine, every last bit of you," and he began to kiss the curve in my neck. His hands wandered over my body and I felt my body reacting. He paused to look in my eyes.

"I like owning you. One day I'm going to own you properly and nobody will stop us then. I want to live with you. Then every day we can be together."

A glimmer of doubt passed through my mind. Did I really want this man owning me? What if he isn't the one? 'It's too late for that now,' said a voice in my head. 'You're a soiled dove. You might as well stay where you are and make the best of it. Anyway, he loves you. Nothing bad will happen.' I let myself relax. After all, this was exciting.

Jumping in the car, two missed calls showed up on my

phone. I knew who they were from without looking. A glance at the time showed I should have been home and hour ago at least. Guilt made me fasten the seatbelt and speed home as fast as I could.

"I was getting worried about you, where have you been?" Mum said as I came through the door.

"Sorry Mum, a parent was late picking up a child, their train was delayed I should have called, I forgot."

The lie slipped out so easily. They came quicker and faster now. The more you lie the more believable they seem to become and the feeling of guilt lessens. It would have been so easy for Mum to ring the nursery where I worked and then the lie would crumble like a house of cards.

How much longer could this continue? I felt a stab of pain as I watched my mum lay aside her knitting and set about getting my tea ready. The ever-present apron tied around her waist, added to the homeliness and comfort of the scene and I wished I could tell Mum everything.

The weekend arrived and I felt a sense of relief as I packed my bag ready to go to my sister Becca's house for a visit. I loved to spend time with my newly married sister and looked forward to the imminent shopping trip that no doubt would happen while Steve, her poor husband, would be on call for work. Kissing both parents goodbye, I sped away in my little KA, enjoying the sense of freedom. I was starting to get nervous about Fred's persistent mentions of getting a place together. It was only last night that he had threatened to tell my parents about our relationship if I didn't soon come clean myself. I suspected they knew something was going on from the questions they had been asking and the look of mistrust in my dad's eyes every time I returned from an evening out or a spontaneous trip to "Tina's house". Time was running out; Fred's threats were far from empty and his temper was beginning to rear its head. The previous weekend he'd bought himself a new phone after smashing his old one into the wall after I said I wasn't ready yet to move in. I was getting more and more tangled in his web and the way out was becoming harder and harder to find. Hopefully this break away would do me good and maybe he would give me some space.

Three

The sun was glinting through the trees and glimpses of new lambs could be seen through the gateways at intervals. A familiar song came on the stereo and Becca turned up the volume as I joined in with the words. We laughed together, Becca taking her hands off the steering wheel to do the actions and quickly returning them as a bend in the road approached. It felt good to be able to be myself. We reminisced about the times Mum and Dad would go on holiday and we would enjoy pigging out on food and watching films in the evenings together while they were away. I thought back to those days and wished I could return to them. Return to that life where there were no secrets or lies, where I knew my parents trusted me and life was simple. If only I could have a fresh start, there would be so many things I would have done differently.

A phone beeped.

"Is that yours?" asked Becca.

My heart sank. Did I really have to look? I put my hand reluctantly in my bag. Of course, it was mine.

"Who is it?" said Becca, never being one to beat about the bush.

Should I tell her? Would Becca understand? Maybe this is the way forward; if I tell her she might tell me what to do. Maybe what I'm doing isn't so bad.

"Hang on, give me chance to look," I replied trying to bluff my way out of it. "It's probably just one of those adverts."

Reluctantly pulling my phone out of my bag, I have a look. My heart sinks. 'Hey, what are you up to? I really miss you. Am just lying on my bed thinking about you, wishing you were here. I'm imaging life with you by my side.'

My stomach does a flip and despite the bright sunshine, the day suddenly feels grey and cold.

"Come on then, who is it?"

"Well if you really wanna know, it's a guy."

Becca immediately turns to look at me, a big smile on her face. "Really? Tell me more!"

"Look where you're going!" I shriek out. I can't help but laugh at my sister's reaction.

"What's he like? Do I know him?"

"Calm down, it's not quite as simple as that." Sobering up I look back down at the text; how shall I say this and how much shall I say?

"He's a guy I went to college with."

Becca lets out a slow "okay and waits for more information. When nothing comes, she asks,

"Does he go to church?"

"No," I reply and my heart feels like its suddenly hardening up, "and this is the problem, there are no chapel going guys around. I can't help it if the only people I see don't go to chapel. I'm never going to find a good chapel boy like you did. I've never done anything the right way so I might as well carry on doing things wrong." Feeling angry, I knew my response was unkind and Becca was undeserving of it but I couldn't help myself. Feeling bitter and guilty, I turned to look at the passing houses out of the window, knowing we were nearing the shops and I could soon find a distraction again.

Becca wisely let the silence rest for a minute, then carefully said, "You could always ask him to come with you to chapel, you never know it might do some good, lots of people marry people that have never been to church."

I thought for a minute. "I don't think he would come."

"If he liked you enough, he would come. Some people might say he would be going for the wrong reasons, just to please you but I think at least he would be there. You never know what could happen. I'll pray about it for you."

'Yes,' I thought, 'you pray because God might listen to you. He doesn't listen to me and you don't know how far into this situation I am'.

The rest of the weekend passed without event and before I knew it, I was back home and Monday morning had arrived.

"Did you have a nice weekend?" asked Mum as she bent down to load the washing machine. She stood and picked up two cups of tea and put one into my hand.

"Yes, thank you," I said brightly. "We went shopping and I bought a new skirt. I'll show you later. What did you get up to?"

Mum replied, "We went for a walk at Ampthill, and then called in to see Grandad Baker. He said he missed you and wanted to know where you were. He might ring later, he's got a tune he wants you to play."

I smiled, this had become a regular thing, Grandad would ring with a hymn tune out of the Companion Tune Book that he wanted me to play over the phone to him, he would then say how much he wished he could play and the conversation continued in the same way it did each time.

"He's becoming more forgetful again and didn't want to go up the road for Chloe's birthday."

Chloe was my cousin who lived up the road from Grandad Baker my mum's dad who had been a widower for many years. In recent days he had stopped calling to visit Chloe and her family.

A twinge of sadness came over me on hearing this and I knew that I should make the most of Grandad.

"I think I will ring him when I get home," I told Mum.

"Yes, he would like that, he still keeps telling me you are going to marry and have lots of children. I don't know why he keeps saying that."

I smiled picturing my grandad in his chair with his feet up on the threadbare stool which he refused to replace, holding his cup of tea in one hand and gripping tight to my hand with the other. He always insisted on holding my hand, running his work-worn fingers over the back of it whilst singing made up songs.

I sighed and smiled at the picture. 'Maybe there's some truth in what he says. Maybe I will have lots of children. I hope the marriage part hurries up!'

"He gave us some pheasants, so we've got one for tea," Mum mentioned

I jerked back to the present with a start and groaned.

Mum smiled, knowing pheasant was my least favourite meal and said brightly, "I'm putting it in some red wine sauce so it will taste better."

I turned and headed upstairs to get ready for work.

As the day at work drew to a close, I said goodbye to the last parent and child and turned to pick up the toys from the floor. I enjoyed my job in the nursery and knew that I would sleep well tonight. It had been a particularly busy day with several staff off sick. Collecting my belongings, I headed out the door hunting through my bag for my keys. Suddenly I stumbled into somebody. Stepping back hastily, I apologized "I'm so sorry I wasn't looking…"

I stopped.

"Fred, what are you doing here?"

"I thought I would surprise you."

I swallowed and paused. My surprise must have shown on my face.

"I thought you would be pleased to see me, what's wrong?"

"Nothing, nothing," I quickly stuttered.

"I'm just surprised that's all, I wasn't expecting to see you."

"I thought you could come back to mine and I'll cook for you."

He puts his arms around my waist and my mind starting planning how I was going to explain to my parents why I was late. I knew they were expecting me for tea so I needed to have an explanation. It was getting exhausting, all of this pretending.

"I'm tired. I don't think tonight will be a good idea. I think I might need an early night."

Fred's face took on a different countenance and he frowned and gripped me tighter. I struggled to step back and he reluctantly let go.

"Typical," he said in a dissatisfied voice. "I don't know why you let your parents dictate to you so much, you're your own person, you should be free to do what you want. I can give you freedom, it's yours if you want it. You've just got to be brave enough to take it."

I sighed and knew he was referring to us moving in together sometime. Maybe it would be an easier option. I thought about my parents and knew that it was chapel night tonight. It was going to be a rush anyway now to make it back in time and besides, they will be preoccupied with chapel they wouldn't be so bothered about where I was.

Fred tried a different tactic and ran a hand down my cheek.

"You are beautiful you know. I'm so lucky to have you, nobody understands me like you do."

I felt my heart softening and smiled. I couldn't help it. Nobody ever called me beautiful. It felt kind of nice.

"Ok hang on, let me just text my mum."

Fred picked me up and swung me round, setting me back on my feet.

"You won't regret it, I promise. I'll make sure you won't."

It was late. I turned the key in the lock. Stepping into the dark hall I made my way up the stairs. My parents' bedroom light was still on. I groaned inwardly.

"Are you alright?" came Mum's voice from the room.

"Yes, thank you," I replied, dumping my bag on my bed.

"Did you have a good day? Come and talk to us."

I sighed. This was all I needed. I'd already sprayed myself with perfume in the car hoping that it would disguise the smell of Fred's aftershave. I was terrified they would find out. Checking myself in the mirror I went into my parents' room. Popping my head around the door I looked in. They were both sat up in bed reading.

"Did you have a good time with Allison?"

"Yes, thank you."

"Where did you go for dinner?"

"Oh, just to the carvery." More lies. When would it end?

Quickly changing the subject

"How was chapel?" I asked.

"It was Mr Cordle. He was really good. He asked after you." The guilt washed over me and for the first time that night I reflected on my actions of the day and began to regret them. I shoved them out of my mind, as I was in the habit of doing.

"I had better get to bed, I'm on an early tomorrow, night, night."

Escaping as quickly as I could, I hurriedly got ready for bed and climbed under the duvet. As I lay back my phone buzzed. Without looking I knew who it would be. I've only been home five minutes and he can't leave me alone.

'I miss you already, can't wait till I next see you. I hope you have sweet dreams. Have just been looking on the internet, think I've found us a house. Will show it to you tomorrow.'

A feeling of dread settled over me. I felt trapped. Part of me wanted to come clean to my parents but I was scared of what their reaction would be. If only I could turn back time.

Putting my phone down, I spotted my Bible on my bedside table. Instead of picking it up I turned out the light and lay down. As soon as my head hit the pillow I remembered something. Grandad. I hadn't rung him. A tear escaped from my eyes and ran down the side of my face. I had let him down.

August 2008

"I've found us the perfect house." Fred was holding a piece of paper with a photo of a house on. I leant over to have a closer look. It did look nice.

"It's got off-road parking for two cars which is ideal and hard to find in the area." I could hear the excitement in his voice. Maybe it wouldn't be so bad having our own house. I took a closer look at the picture of the kitchen. I could imagine myself cooking dinner and washing up looking out over the garden. Isn't this what I had always wanted? Surely in time, my family would come around to the idea and who knows, they might even come for tea. Now that would be great.

"I've booked a viewing for tomorrow. You finish at six, don't you? So I've booked it for half six."

I didn't have time to respond before Fred continued.

"All we need to think about is getting a deposit together. How much money have you got saved?" I swallowed; this was moving too fast. I thought about the money I'd managed to save since starting work. That money was for the future, my dad had said when he had helped me open a savings account. Was this what my future was meant to be? And what would he think if I used the money in this way? Somehow, I felt as though I should speak to him before making any decisions. Looking at the price of renting the property, I did some sums in my head and knew we could manage the payments, but I had doubts at spending my money on renting.

"Is it not better if we slow down a bit? If we tell my parents, give them time to get to know you and we can start saving for a house. I just feel that renting is wasting money."

"Deb, you know your parents will never accept me and besides, why wait?"

The house was lovely and just what I had dreamed of. What's more, it was hidden away down a dead-end street so I was sure my family wouldn't be able to find me. I was persuaded.

So, I ran. Ran from my family into the arms of Fred. I ran, escaping from the constraints of family life. Mum and Dad were away on holiday, which gave me the perfect opportunity to pack up my life and scribble a note. I can only imagine how they must have felt when they returned from their holiday to find me gone. It didn't take Dad long to track me down, just a matter of hours. I've no idea how he did it but it shows how much he loved me. But my mind was made up, Fred had won me over.

I had moved out previously, but had been persuaded to move back home by my family. Home I returned to Mum and Dad. Becca and her husband Steve were at Mum and Dad's and they were helping to bring my stuff back in from the car. Steve was on one of his trips up the stairs with a load of stuff, and he enveloped me in a big bear hug. Tears came to my eyes. 'Maybe this was where I belong' I had thought. But the pull of Fred was too strong and the life out there too exciting, so this time I cut off all ties with my family and ran away again. There was no going back now.

Four

I was upstairs getting ready. We were off out to a car cruise in Milton Keynes. I really didn't want to go. Downstairs in our living room were several of our friends. Well... I say "our friends", I didn't really consider them to be my friends. I could hear their voices and laughter drifting up the stairs. I sat down on the edge of the bed. Maybe I could say I didn't feel well and stay here. We had been living together for about a year now. It was nice to have some independence but things hadn't turned out exactly how I had expected them to.

"Are you ready?" called Fred.

Wearily getting up, I headed down the stairs. "Hi!" I said with forced brightness.

It was a Sunday evening and I couldn't help but wonder what my family were doing. It had been so long since I had been to church that I had forgotten what that 'Sunday feeling' felt like and most of the time I didn't even give a thought to what a Sunday used to be like.

We headed out the door and I sat in the passenger seat of Fred's bright orange modified Ford Focus. He drove fast. I liked that. It was exciting. I began to forget my family and enjoy the ride. The deep bass of the music coming from the sub in the boot made my insides vibrate and I enjoyed the feeling. When we pulled into the cruise everybody turned and stared. Fred wound the windows down and turned the music up. He liked the attention. People stopped their conversations to turn and stare at us. I was never sure where to look, not liking the attention. I was glad when we parked and I could get out. People surrounded the car and I moved to the back of the crowd. I felt so alone. I looked at the couples surrounding the car. The guys stood behind the girls with their arms around their waists whispering in their ears. 'Where was Fred?' I wondered feeling a stab of loneliness. I stood on tiptoe and looked over the heads of the spectators. The music was making the floor vibrate and the crowds loved it, some people were dancing, while others stood at the back of the car watching somebody's phone bounce on the huge speaker. Fred was sat in the front seat and next to him sat a tall blonde girl with a skirt so short it even made me blink. The air from the sub was making her hair blow and Fred was smiling at her. The crowd laughed and the girl got out and swapped with another. I felt so alone. Nobody would notice if I just walked away, least of all Fred. I spotted one of the older members of the cruise and made my way over to talk to him. He wasn't drawn in with the loud music. It was nice to get away from it. He lit a cigarette and asked how I was doing. After about half an hour Fred came looking for me,

"We're going to get something to eat, are you coming?" he asked.

"Sure," I replied.

"What's wrong with you?" he sighed.

"Nothing," I sulkily replied. I couldn't be bothered to talk to him.

Several hours later we were alone on our way home.

"I think I might get a new battery for the sub." I didn't reply but kept silent.

"Deb!" he shouted. "Did you hear what I said?"

"Yes, I heard you."

"Why aren't you saying anything then?"

"What do you want me say?" I quickly replied. "You do whatever you want anyway, so I don't know why you're telling me."

"Ah come on, don't be like that, what is wrong? Tell me and I can make it better." He reached out to touch me and I shoved him away, really not wanting to be touched.

I was angry.

"You think you can sit in this car and chat up other girls and then five minutes later sweet talk me… your girlfriend? Forget it, mate, I don't think so! You looked very comfortable earlier with those other girls, you didn't even realise where I was."

"Deb, that's not true, those girls are nothing compared with you, I didn't do anything, everyone came to me, I didn't do anything".

"Puhhh," I replied sarcastically. "No, you just drove in with your music blaring basically shouting 'look at me, everyone'!"

"And what were you doing, Deb? Talking to Ray, chatting him up I suppose. And yes, I did see you even though you think I didn't."

I laughed. I couldn't help myself. Ray was old enough to be my dad!

My eyes felt tired and I didn't want to argue any more. Fred said something but I didn't hear him. My mind was far away. I was imagining a different life. Several times I had imagined myself married. Not to Fred though, but somebody else. I had no image of the man who was my imaginary husband, except that he was kind and gentle. I let my imagination wander and pictured him coming home from work and giving me a hug, asking how my day had gone. Somewhere deep down, I knew that I wouldn't be with Fred forever I just needed to figure out a way of getting away from him.

I was tired. It had been a long week at work. My head was pounding from the head cold I'd been struggling to shake. I was looking forward to having a soak in a hot bubbly bath. Staff had been off sick and I'd clocked up fifty-seven hours. Arriving home, I unlocked the front door. Fred was lying on the sofa. It looked like he'd been there a long time. He didn't bother to get up.

"Alright?" I said.

"No, not really," he grouched in reply.

"What's up?" I asked.

"I've lost my job."

I was shocked. It took a few seconds for me to take it in.

"Why?" I stammered.

A stream of curses spewed out of his mouth along with a recount of his run-in with a fellow farm labourer. It turned out that Fred had lost his temper and ended up kicking his colleague's car, leaving a dent, resulting in instant dismissal. Fear curled its way around my spine. I had to get away from this toxic situation.

It was late. I rolled over in bed for the hundredth time. A car pulled into the street.

'Is it him?' It carried on past the house. Reaching for my phone I had a look at the time. 3 a.m. I sat up and had a drink of water. 'Where is he? What's he doing?' This wasn't the first time he was home much later than he said he would be. I sighed and snuggled back down closing my eyes willing sleep to come.

At 4 a.m. the front door went. Fred crept up the stairs and went to use the bathroom. I turned over as he got into bed.

"Where have you been?" I asked.

"I told you, we've been out for dinner."

"I know that but you said it wouldn't be a late one."

"We went into town and then I took everyone home."

A feeling of dread settled itself into the pit of my stomach. Something wasn't right. He wasn't telling the truth. His voice sounded different. I thought back over the last month to the other times I'd had this feeling. I knew it was useless to ask more and really didn't feel like getting into an argument. Last time I had confronted him, it had ended in a full-blown row and a punched door. Closing my eyes, I thought back over the last year. It was all so exciting and new, last August when we had picked the keys and set foot in our new home. I remembered how he'd swung me round and told me how much the house suited me and how happy we would be. The freedom was fun and it was nice to have our own place. As the months passed, reality began to set in. The job loss hadn't helped, resulting in me working extra hours and after long days coming home to a messy house and Fred spread out over the sofa.

But then, when a new job came along things went from bad to worse and that's when the late nights and mysterious phone calls started to happen. A snore came from the other side of the bed. I slid away and stared at a mark on the wall. A tear slid down my cheek onto the pillow. I'd been such an idiot. How could I have been so blind. Morning couldn't come quick enough.

At last 8.00 came and I got up leaving a sleeping Fred sprawled in bed. I went to the kitchen to put the kettle on and was greeted by Keira's furry face and wet tongue. Sliding to the floor, I buried my face in the dog's soft fur and put my arms around her neck. Keira sniffed my head and looked at me with her head on the side as if to ask what was wrong. Smiling, I rubbed between her ears and remembered when we had gone to pick her up a few months before and how tiny she was. She'd slept the whole way home curled up on my lap. The dog lay down across my knees, giving a big sigh. Taking a moment to reflect, I knew that today was the day I was going to pack my bags and leave. I was scared of what his reaction would be but knew if I waited any longer, I would chicken out. Keira shuffled on my lap and I tried to figure out if there was any room in my plan for her but knew there wasn't. There was no way I could take her with me, I didn't even know where I was going to go yet. I would miss the dog but knew it was for the best. Besides, Keira wasn't even half grown yet and she was already looking massive, her big paws hanging down off my leg. Footsteps sounded on the stairs and I rose and finished making my tea. Fred came in and put his arm around me. I drew back and hastily made my way up the stairs, tears springing into my eyes. I tried to swallow them away. I had to be strong. The very touch of him made anger boil inside me. How dare he touch me.

"What's wrong with you?" came the accusing tone as I turned to face him.

"I think you know."

"Know what?"

"I know that you've been lying to me. I don't know what you've been up to, but I think you're seeing someone else. There's no point arguing. I'm packing my stuff and then you're free to carry on whatever you're doing without me getting in the way."

The tears had disappeared and a deep-seated rage was beginning to rise up inside the pit of my stomach.

Fred was taken aback by my tone and followed me up the stairs. He sat on the bed as I opened the wardrobe doors and pulled out a bag. I began grabbing clothes and shoving them into the case. Fred leaned forward and tried to grab my arm.

"Get your hand off me. I don't want you anywhere near me, you disgust me, and to think that I thought you loved me." The anger began to consume me blurring my vision and thoughts. Slamming a door shut I turned and crashed into Fred's chest. Looking up into his eyes I saw a mirror of my own anger. Fear clutched at my insides and took root in the bottom of my stomach like a cold wind. I wondered how close he was to hitting me.

Grabbing both arms, he flung me onto the bed and pinned me down, leaning over me.

"I won't let you leave," he stuttered. "You're mine and always will be."

I forced my body to relax, knowing if I did his vice-like grip would release me. Trying another tactic, he began to gently run his hand along the side of my body. Bile rose in my mouth and I managed to sit up and swallow hard. Seizing the opportunity, I rolled over and slid off the bed to resume my packing. Fred sat and watched me silently and I savoured the silence using it to gather myself together. Shrugging his shoulders, he sat back and watched me laughing. His mocking laugh made me shiver as it was full of contempt.

"So, where you gonna go then? Your family won't want you. I'll be surprised if you even last the day."

I looked up in surprise at this change of tactic. Doubt began to creep in. He was right, I had nowhere to go and there was no way I could turn up at my parents' door. I'd already made my choice and pride wouldn't let me admit that my parents had been right. The sad truth settled on me like a black cloud. It was ridiculous thinking I could make it alone.

"Stay here with me and we will sort things out." I glanced at him and could see he was trying again with renewed vigour, obviously feeding off my uncertainty.

For a moment I pictured a different life with a different man. A man who went to church. A man who got on well with my family. This was not the first time I had dreamt of a different life. Maybe there's hope if I get out now, maybe I still have time to start again. With a resolve to leave, I picked up my suitcase and headed for the door.

Fred remained sitting on the bed.

"Bye then," he said casually.

I felt the anger rising but pushed it down and walked out the front door my head held high. I flung my case in the boot of my car, and sped away giving the engine an extra rev.

Driving without seeing, I tried to put distance between myself and what I had just come from. Spotting a sign for a lay-by I took the turning right and pulled over. Turning off the engine I buried my head in my hands and my body began to shake as the sobs came one after the other. The realisation of what I had just done began to sink in. Anger swept through me and I reached up and punched the ceiling of the car before dissolving again into a heap of tears. "Why, oh why?" I cried into the empty car. "Why has this happened to me?" My head began to pound as the tears streamed down my face and there seemed to be no end to the heartache that consumed me.

As the time passed the tears began to slow and my vision began to clear. My stomach rumbled and I remembered I'd not eaten breakfast. Head thumping, I glanced at the dashboard clock. It read 11.00 a.m. Wondering what to do next, I decided to call my friend Bella from work. Maybe I could go and see her. She might even have a spare bed for the night.

A few hours later I sat down hard on the bed in a Travelodge room. Bella didn't offer a bed and I hadn't liked to ask. The room was bare, and I felt the reality of my situation beginning to sink in. Looking for a distraction I searched for the TV remote. It wasn't on the bedside table or on the cabinet next to the TV. Frustration began to build and tears blurred my vision. I hunted in every other possible place in the room without success. Grabbing the room key, I headed down to the reception. It was late and the lady behind the desk looked up, irritated at the interruption.

"Can I help?"

"Yes please, I can't find the TV remote in my room."

"That's because we don't provide them, you can pay extra to have one."

The room itself had already cost £45 and I was unsure of how many more nights I needed.

"I'll give it a miss, thanks." I didn't have the energy to argue and turned to return to the room. Turing the TV on by hand, I got ready for bed and settled down for a fitful night's sleep.

The next morning dawned bringing with it a headache and aching limbs. Sitting up, I realised the TV had been droning away all night. It was Sunday and my thoughts turned to my family. It had been a long time since I had thought about the old Sunday routine and I sat and wondered what they were doing. The thought came to mind of turning up at church and just sitting at the back. As soon as the thought arrived, I dismissed it. Imagine how people would whisper behind their hands and pretend not to stare. I looked so different to the girl they used to know. My once curly brown hair was now used to the regular straightening and the new copper highlights were beginning to grow out. What would they think of me? How could I face them now? It was a silly idea. With the realisation it was Monday tomorrow, I began to think about the week ahead. My boss was very friendly and understanding so I decided to give her a call. True to form she soon answered and didn't mind being bothered on a Sunday.

Bev answered after the third ring, "Hi Deb, how you doing?"

I took a deep breath and talked her through the last twelve hours. Fifteen minutes later I put the phone down and breathed a sigh of relief. Bev had said her mum had a spare room in her house and I was welcome to stay there until I was sorted. The situation certainly wasn't ideal but it was a lot cheaper!

Five

Parking was difficult down the side streets where Bev's mum, Paula lived. I concentrated on not hitting the car behind as I completed my parallel park. It made me feel nauseous when I looked up at the terraced houses and felt sure I could remember a time when my grandad Baker had driven me down these very roads and shown me where Grandma used to live. The houses looked small from the front but once inside they went back a long way with lovely long gardens. It had been three days since I'd moved in. Paula had been very kind but she insisted on cooking for me as well as herself. Eating was proving difficult and I was finding it increasingly harder to try and choke down the lovely meals she had prepared. It seemed every time I attempted to eat, Fred's face appeared in my mind.

The next day was Sunday. I had hardly slept and felt the urge to go and see Fred. I rose, showered and dressed then drove around there. I pulled across the bottom of the drive. There was another car there next to his. I ignored it and went to the front door. Using my key, I tried to unlock the door. The key wouldn't turn. I felt anger. This was my house and I was locked out. I banged on the door and waited. There was a scuffling and banging around from inside. The door finally opened. Fred stood there he had obviously just got out of bed.

"Can I come in?" I asked. He looked surprised and just stared at me. I tried to push past him into the hall way but he blocked the way.

"Er... no," he said.

"It's my house too. Let me in."

"Do you want to see Keira?" Fred said quickly.

"Yes," I said, thinking he would change his mind and let me in.

"Hang on then."

He reached for his keys and unlocked his car.

"There, you can sit in there."

I turned, giving up on being let in and got into his car. A minute later, the car door opened and Keira jumped in, followed by Fred. She was very excited and jumped onto my lap. Her tail was wagging knocking into anything that got in its way. She stood on my lap nearly crushing me and licked my face. Her nose was wet and I tried to dry my face on my arm. I smiled as I tried to fight her off but she was so persistent. Laughingly, I pushed her away, struggling for breath. She wouldn't be put off and tried to push her doggy nose against me again. This time her head collided with my lip and I felt warm blood and began to taste it. I pushed her away more firmly and felt my lip with my hand. My hand came away red. She had split my lip in her enthusiasm. Keira sat down in the footwell of the car on top of my feet and stayed there looking up at me. I pulled the sun visor down to have a look in the mirror. My lip was badly split and was already beginning to swell. The blood was starting to make its way down my chin and I caught it in my hand as it dripped. I looked to Fred, hoping he would help me. He had his head turned away and was looking out the window.

"Do you have a tissue?" I asked.

He turned to look at me and shook his head.

There I was with a swelling lip and blood pouring down my face and all he could do was stare at me. I was shocked. I thought at least he would go inside and get a tissue. His eyes were cold as he looked at me and I knew in that instant that he didn't love me, I felt such a deep feeling of sadness. I mopped up as best I could with an old tissue I found in my pocket and decided to ask why I couldn't go inside.

"You just can't," he said.

Even though I knew deep down he didn't love me, I still felt like I needed to hear it from him before I gave up hope. Besides, I was the one who had dumped him. It should have been him begging for me back. I knew that any more conversation would have been pointless so I got out of the car and walked towards my own. The tears streamed down my face and the familiar pounding started in my head. I had cried more in the last few days more than I could ever remember.

December 2009

I had been to look around several rooms available to rent. Most of them were the spare bedroom in a family home and I couldn't seem to settle on one. The prospect of living in a family home without being part of the family saddened me. The loneliness of my situation became more and more apparent and yet my foolish pride wouldn't allow me pick up the phone and call my parents. It was early December and Christmas was fast approaching. Bev's mum assured me I could stay as long as I needed but I was feeling the need for my own space. I slammed the car door shut and let myself in the front door. I was surprised to see a group of people sitting in a circle in Paula's front room. Paula introduced them as her friends from church. She explained they were having a Bible study and would I like to join in. Bitterness rose up inside me and I felt a sneer creeping up onto my face. I managed to push it down and replied in what I hoped was a civilized manner. As quick as I could, I climbed the stairs to my room and shut the door. Bible study! They must have been having a joke. After all this time away from home, trying to get away from church and all that went with it and here I was in my room with a Bible study going on downstairs! I could imagine them all sitting there being told about my situation and feeling sorry for me and perhaps even praying for the troubled soul upstairs. Well, I thought they could keep their prayers. I didn't need them. I could cope just fine on my own. I was angry. I lay down on my bed and reached for my phone. Scrolling through every picture from the last year or so I went through and deleted every one. The tears ran down my face and dripped onto the screen. Angrily swiping them away, I reached a picture of Keira sitting there with her puppy eyes looking up at me.

I fell back on the bed and sobbed. I had no one. Not even my dog for comfort.

The extent of my misery was about to worsen. It had been a few months previously that I had received a letter in the post regarding a speeding fine. I was required to attend a court date which was fast approaching. In my head I wanted to have a place to live sorted before the court date. I was due to go and view a room in a house with my colleague after work.

We pulled up outside the large grey-looking building. We parked the car and walked to find the front door. A smart-looking Asian man greeted us at the door.

"Deb?" he asked.

"Yes," I replied and gave him my hand to shake.

"Come in," he said.

We followed him in and he began to show us around. Whilst showing us the room, he asked questions about what job I did and explained to me that he rented out the rooms to young professionals. The room was small and was very close to the communal bathroom. He explained that he had another room available that was a bit bigger and had a sink in it. We had a look and instantly I felt more at home. It was a lot bigger and felt lighter. There was even a wardrobe and a big double bed. I asked how much it would be and he replied "£450 a month".

£450 a month! I was shocked. I pretended to be calm and asked if I could have the contract on a month by month basis. Somewhere in my head I knew this situation wouldn't be permanent and wanted to make sure I wasn't tied in. The owner said that it wasn't something he normally did but he would make an exception this time.

"Now about the price" I said not used to haggling but knowing that I had no choice. "Will you take anything less?"

He looked at me and smiled and I had a small attempt at giving him a cute smile. Anything to save some money.

"You can have it for £400 a month."

"Great!" I replied and shook his hand. I breathed a sigh

of relief. £400 was my limit. The smile must have worked. We agreed that I would move in on the Saturday and he even offered to meet me there to help unload my car. I felt relieved that things were beginning to get sorted out.

The move went well and my new landlord was very helpful. A bit too helpful. I sat in my new room looking around at my few belongings. There had been a note pushed under my new bedroom door from my new housemates welcoming me. This made me feel better and I was looking forward to meeting them. It was nice to have my own space but part of me still felt empty and unsure. I had arranged to go and meet my sister Becca the next morning and then later on I was going to see Fred. I thought if I could just see him then maybe we could sort things out. In my foolish heart I still wanted to repair our relationship. My tummy rumbled and I released that I had hardly eaten anything over the past few days.

I sat in Becca's car. We were in a lay-by just outside the village where the church I used to attend was. It was Sunday and she would soon be off to the service. She tried to persuade me to come with her but I told her that I had arranged to meet Fred.

"What for?" she asked.

"So, we can talk and sort things out. We are going to take Keira for a walk together."

"Do you want to sort things out?"

I shrugged, not sure what to say. My sister was several months pregnant and I was very excited. Part of me knew that if I was to repair things with Fred, then I wouldn't see very much of my niece or nephew and this made me sad. I knew that he was a barrier between me and my family. This new life was so precious and I felt like it was telling me that I could have another chance. Part of me wanted to stay with Becca and go back to my old life but I'm ashamed to say that the tug of Fred was stronger. I left her that day with the promise I would stay in touch. My mum had always said to us, "Never fall out... you promise me you will never fall out".

Six

The morning of my court date arrived. I felt so nervous. What should I wear? I put on a straight black skirt and cream blouse, hoping I looked professional. Standing in front of the mirror in my rented room, I eyed the black circles under my eyes. I hadn't slept a wink. It hadn't helped that I had staked out the house I had shared with Fred last night, to see what was going on. He hadn't arrived home until 2 a.m. At least he had been on his own. Where had he been until that time on a Sunday night?

My friend from London had come up for the weekend and kept me company. We had gone to a cruise in Northampton on the Sunday evening. I had hoped for a glimpse of Fred and that's exactly what I'd got. Except he wasn't on his own; in his car there was a blonde girl sat next to him. I felt sick when I saw her sat in the seat where I normally sat. How dare she? As soon as I had seen them, I wanted to tear her out of the car and punch Fred right in his smug face. My suspicions had been confirmed. I called one of his friends to find out who she was and was told she was somebody he worked with. I was beginning to realise how alone I was and wished I could go back to living with him. I was willing to forgive him if only we could just start again. Anything to take away this feeling of loneliness. I felt so angry and grasped how much I had thrown away and how little I had left.

My friend drove me to the court to help take some of the pressure off me. We sat together in a sort of waiting room, watching the people coming and going. I couldn't stop my legs from bouncing up and down and I kept picking my fingers.

An official looking lady walked in with a clip board and called out a list of names. "Mr Jones, Mr Miles, Mr Matthews, Mr Dawson, Mr Witsome…"

One by one the men got up and followed her out of the

room. I breathed a sigh and carried on waiting.

"Are you sure that wasn't for you?" asked my friend.

"I didn't hear my name," I replied.

"No but she said Mr Dawson, what if she got it wrong?"

'Great' I thought, now I've gone and missed court as well. My friend went and chased after her. After several minutes he returned.

"Quick," he said, "it was for you. Hurry, we can catch them up."

I quickly gathered up our stuff and followed after them. We went up a wide staircase and down gilded halls to another waiting room where we continued to wait. I looked around at the other people waiting and felt so out of place being the only girl and the only young one at that. A name was called and a scruffy-looking gentleman got up and followed a lady out. 'At least I look smart' I thought to myself. After a short period, the scruffy-looking man reappeared. This time he looked angry and red in the face. A flow of angry, unrepeatable words left his mouth and I surmised by what he said that the judge was a lady. Several more men were called and left until finally it was my turn.

I followed a lady into the court room and was directed to stand in the dock. There was a chair in there, which I assumed was for me and I eagerly sank into it. An urgent and hushed voice came from behind me.

"Stand up."

Which I quickly did. A dark wooden door opened at the front of the room and a smart, and serious looking lady walked through. The court was told to sit, but I was to remain standing. My mind was in a daze and I was unsure of what was happening. At one point the judge asked me if there was any way I would be able to get a bus to work. I nodded, too scared to say otherwise. After a while the judge stood up and went back through the door that she had previously entered. I was confused but all I could do was wait. It felt like ages until she finally reappeared. They had made their decision. I was to be fined and be suspended from driving for twenty-five days. I felt sick. My first thought was work, how was I going to get there? In a daze I was led out of the court room and reunited with my friend. I decided to pay the fine there and then and headed straight downstairs to pay. It was at the little office, which was more like a small hatch in the wall, that they took my driving license away and I filled out a form.

As soon as we left the building the tears began to flow. I was ruined. I didn't know where to go or what to do. I asked my friend to take me back to the house that Fred and I had shared. I wanted to have it out with him once and for all.

My key working this time, I let myself in the front door and I was greeted by Keira. She was so excited to see me and ran into my legs, almost tripping me up. I knelt down and gave her a massive cuddle and she rubbed her soft puppy head against mine. Bounding off, she fetched a toy thinking it was play time. I told her "in a minute", and decided to have a look around the house. Fred wasn't home so I was free to wander. It felt strange to walk up the stairs feeling like an intruder. I remembered the first time I had walked down the stairs and he had stood at the bottom. He had picked me up and spun me round telling me how much the house suited me. I was happy then. Well, at least I thought I was. I shook my head as if to get rid of the memory and made my way into the bedroom we had shared. I don't know what I was looking for but I felt I needed to open the wardrobe door and look inside. There hung my clothes next to his. Part of me wanted to lift the bed covers but I wasn't sure what I was looking for. The front door went. I froze. What should I do? I felt sick. I slowly walked down the stairs. Fred was bent down giving Keira's head a rub.

"Hello," I said cautiously.

He hadn't noticed me and jumped when he saw me.

"What are you doing here?"

"I've come to see you. We need to talk."

"What about?"

"Us," I replied.

"What do you mean 'us'? There is no 'us'."

I sat on the stairs and Keira came and put her head on my lap.

"I shouldn't do that," said Fred, addressing the dog. "You don't know where she's been."

"What do you mean I don't know where she's been? I'm not the one who's been sleeping around, and don't lie to me, I know you have."

Fred didn't reply but calmly sat on the sofa and turned the TV on.

"Have you got anything to say?"

Fred just shrugged.

I felt like I was getting nowhere.

"I just want to know why, why didn't you just talk to me. We could have figured it out. Why didn't you speak to me, I thought you loved me?"

Finally, Fred turned to look at me and I was surprised by how cold his pale blue eyes looked.

"You never did understand me, Deb. How do I know that you haven't been seeing someone behind my back?"

I was shocked. How could he think that?

"I gave up everything for you and this is how you repay me." I was angry; there was no stopping me now. "You think it was easy giving up my family. For what, Fred, for what? I am not going to be your toy any more. I am worth more than that. These past few days have taught me that. I don't deserve to be lied to any more."

It suddenly hit me how betrayed my parents must feel and how often I had lied to them. I now had a small understanding of what it felt like to be betrayed. The desire to see them overwhelmed me.

"What happened in court?" asked Fred.

"They took my licence away and I had to pay a fine."

His sadistic laugh rang in my ears. "What are you going to do?"

"As if you care," I replied.

I'd had enough. It was time. I got up to leave.

"Where are you going?"

"Far away from you."

"How? You haven't got a car?"

I stood up and marched out the front door. It was raining. The sort of rain that soaked you in seconds. I didn't care; I just wanted to put distance between us. I walked as fast as I could. The rain blinded my vision until I could hardly see where my feet were falling. I had reached the end of the road and was waiting to cross; when I heard the deep bass sounding exhaust of Fred's car. I ran across the road and into the petrol station. Had he really come to pick me up? A small glimmer of hope rose inside me. Perhaps he really did care. I saw the black bonnet of his car stop briefly at the crossroads and then it pulled away. He hadn't seen me. I searched in my purse to see if I had money for a taxi. I pulled out £10. That should be enough to get to my parents. I called a taxi and thought I'd better warn my parents I was coming. My mum answered after two rings. It was so good to hear her voice. The conversation was brief.

The taxi soon arrived and I gingerly stepped into the back. I felt strangely nervous; I'd never been in a taxi on my own before. The rain grew heavier. There was so much spray we could hardly see where we were going. The wipers of the car sped across the windscreen hardly making any difference. I looked out the window trying to find out where we were and soon noticed the driver was taking the long route. 'Hurry up!' I wanted to scream. After what seemed like some hours' drive but was probably only 20 minutes, we arrived.

"That will be £10," said the driver.

I was shocked. I hadn't expected to lose all of my money. It was literally the only money I had left. Reluctantly I handed it over and jumped out as fast as I could, making a dash through the puddles to my parents' front door.

There's so much I could say about that first meeting with my parents but I don't know where to start. There were many tears and I remember how homely and comforting their house was to me. It wasn't until that moment that I knew that I had missed it. I loved the way so little had changed and I felt comforted by the presence of the familiar furniture and surroundings. Mum had cooked her speciality of potatoes in gravy and I knew there was no other meal I would rather have eaten. To this day, I know I am home when Mum cooks that. After dinner we sat in the lounge and it took very little prompting for me to tell them the whole story. In between floods of tears and sips of tea, my tale of woe came out.

Being my parents, who love me more than I could ever understand, they didn't condemn but were honest and frank whilst being kind. There were no accusations of 'I told you so' but I could tell they were not surprised. After an emotional evening they took me back to the house where I was living and Mum gave me £10 to cover the cost of the taxi. She gave me a bag full of food and I showed them around my room. We parted, agreeing to see each other again soon. That night I climbed into bed relishing the feel of my parents' embrace.

In the days following, I began to come to terms with what Fred had done to me. I couldn't understand why he had done what he had and yet at the same time knew, if he showed enough remorse, I was weak enough to have him back. I was lonely. One evening after work I sat in my room searching through the files on our shared laptop. If there was any evidence of Fred's behaviour, I was sure to find it on there. I came across old conversations he'd had with another girl on MSN Messenger. The things he had been saying to her were not only inappropriate for a guy in a relationship but were also enough to make my blood boil. I'd never felt such hatred. It was one thing knowing that he had been cheating, but to actually have it written down in black and white was another thing altogether. It was a whole other level. I flung my chair on the floor and looked for something to punch or throw. That's it, I thought. I'm going around there. I'm going to get a knife and slash his tyres. I had never felt anger like it. Angrily grabbing my shoes, I pulled them on and then stopped. What was I thinking? I can't go around there. I'm not allowed to drive. I felt like a balloon, with the wind let out of me. Sinking to the floor I pulled my knees up to my chest and dropped my head onto them rocking backwards and forwards. The whole world felt as though it was against me and was laughing at my despair. I now realise that God's hand was on my life. Who knows what would have happened if I had been allowed to drive?

Seven

The New Year brought with it new beginnings. I moved back home after Christmas and after completing my driving ban I eventually got my license back. On the first Saturday morning of the year my dad and brother Tom went with me to the house where Fred and I had lived together and collected my things. Fred had told me that he would be at work, but I was worried he would return and wanted to get out of there as soon as possible. We loaded up my dad's car, barely managing to squeeze everything in and I posted my key through the letter box. Looking back now I realised at the time I was too wrapped up in my own feelings of sadness and melancholy to consider how my dad and brother must have been feeling. What a bittersweet thing for them to have to do.

When we returned home, Mum was at the door to greet us and without saying anything she just wrapped me in one of her hugs. Dad and Tom set about unloading the car, whilst Mum and I started to sort out my things. Amongst the heaps of stuff was my Bible. I placed it next to my bed determined to look at it that night before bed. When evening came I readied for bed and settled down. I opened my Bible, not sure where to turn to. A verse came into my head. It was:

'Jesus saith unto him, I am the way, the truth, and the life: no man cometh unto the Father but by me.'
John 14:6

I turned to John Chapter 14 and the first words I read hit me.

'Let not your heart be troubled: ye believe in God, believe also in me. In my father's house are many

**mansions: if it were not so, I would have told you. I go
to prepare a place for you. And if I go and prepare a
place for you, I will come again, and receive you unto
myself; that where I am, there ye may be also.'
John 14:1-3**

I stopped. The words were like a balm to my broken heart.
I wasn't really sure what they meant but the comfort they
gave was like nothing I'd ever experienced before. Settling
down to sleep I felt safe. It was good to be home.

March 2010

March the 30th was a very special day! My niece was born.
We drove to see her that same day once both mum and baby
were allowed home. The drive over to Oxfordshire seemed
to take twice as long as normal and we stopped halfway to
have a drink somewhere giving the new little family time to
get settled before we arrived. As soon as we had parked,
Mum and I virtually ran up the long path to the house. A
gentle knock at the door was soon answered.
    And there she was.
    Our Kezia.
    Laid in Becca's arms. So tiny. So beautiful.
    Everybody had a cuddle, and I could hardly wait for my
turn.
    As I cradled her tiny body in my arms, I struggled to
keep my emotions at bay. I was not prepared for how much
the moment moved me. To think I could have missed such
a precious occasion. There was nowhere in the world I
would rather have been. Picking up her little hand I stroked
her soft skin and examined her tiny fingers. She was so
perfect and beautiful. I felt such a love for her and the
overwhelming desire to protect her from our cruel world.
She was dressed in a white babygrow and had one of Mum's
hand knitted yellow jumpers on. There was nothing I
wouldn't have done to protect that little girl. In the days to
follow I thought a lot about the love I had for Kezia, and

realised it wasn't as strong as my parents' love for me. It then began to dawn on me the pain and heartache I had caused them and how much my actions had put them through.

As in the days before I had moved away, I began to stay for weekends with my sister Becca and Steve her husband. Steve was still having to take his turn on the call out rota so I would coincide my visits with these weekends to give Becca some company. Of course, these weekends now had a new appeal with the addition of little Kezia. During the day we continued our much-loved shopping expeditions, and as Kezia grew she soon learnt to put up with heaps of clothes laid across her pram.

When the evenings came, we settled down to watch our favourite films, whilst munching on lots of snacks. In the nights when Kezia woke for a feed and Steve was out on call, I would go and sit next to Becca on the bed and talk to her as she tended to Kezia's needs. On one occasion I watched as Becca tenderly laid Kezia back in her Moses basket. I stayed a while just looking at her. Becca exhausted lay down and was soon back to sleep. Kezia, not ready for sleep yet, wriggled around and made soft cooing noises. I peeked over the side of the basket thinking maybe I should go back to bed and let her settle but couldn't resist another look. She made eye contact with me and lifted her feet in the air. I couldn't help but smile. Again, it overwhelmed me, that feeling of love and protectiveness. I let her settle and returned to my own bed.

Another appeal of staying with Becca and Steve, were the Sunday visits to Oxford Chapel. It was good to go to a church where people were not aware of my history and I could blend into the crowd. It was in this little chapel, in the centre of Oxford that the Lord spoke to me on several occasions. It is only now when I look back that I can see God's hand leading and directing me through his word. On one particular visit Mr Morlan, the pastor, preached on the following verse:

**'As far as the east is from the west, so far hath he
removed our transgressions from us.'**
Psalm 103:12

In his usual expressive manner, he pointed first at one wall
of the little chapel and then to the other to emphasise his
point of how far away our sins could be removed from us.
This struck a chord inside me and I really felt as though he
was speaking directly to me. The east and west surely do
not meet, so that must mean that your sins could be removed
totally away from you. I wished deep down inside me that
my sins could be that far away from me but I didn't know
how to get them away. I had tried living in a good way but
I kept on falling. The harder I tried the further I seemed to
fall. My past actions had been keeping me awake at night
as I replayed in my head all the lies I had told and all the
sinful things I had done. I felt very down and disheartened
and really wondered what the future would hold for me.

November 2010

Soon after hearing Mr Morlan's sermon in Oxford, Mr Peter
Rowell came and preached at Westoning, (my mum and
dad's home church). He spoke on the latter part of a verse
in Philippians 3 which reads:

**'this one thing I do, forgetting those things which are
behind, and reaching forth to those things which are
before'.**
Philippians 3 :13

He spoke about when you look back over your life and you
see all the sins you have committed as though they were a
mountain range. Some of the mountains are huge and seem
unpassable and no matter what you do you cannot get over
them. It felt to me as though he was painting a picture of

my life. That is exactly how I'd been feeling. I felt as though there was no getting over my sins and that I would never be rid of them. Mr Rowell continued in his slow and deliberate manner, speaking about the amazing power of God and how he can flatten mountains. He encouraged the listeners not to let the sins of the past get in the way of the future but, when you look back over your life, see God's righteousness in the way He has worked things out.

I felt as though I was only the only person seated in the chapel that day. It was as though Mr Rowell was talking directly to me. My sins were exactly as he had described. Great, big mountains in my memory, and despite what I did there was no getting away from them. I felt as though I was going to have to carry the weight of them with me for my whole life

Mr Rowell then went on to speak on the next verse:

'I press towards the mark for the prize of the high calling of God in Christ Jesus'.
Philippians 3:14

He spoke about the hope of heaven. I had never heard a sermon like it. It was first time I really felt like there was hope for me. After chapel I went to my room and turned in my Bible to John chapter 14:

'I go to prepare a place for you, And if I go and prepare a place for you, I will come again, and receive you unto myself; that where I am, there ye may be also'.
John 14:2,3

I realised that this verse was talking about heaven and that I wanted to go there. In the days and months that followed I spent many hours in God's word reading. I was determined to read the Bible cover to cover. (This was something that took me several years to accomplish.) As the weeks and months past, I came to the understanding, that there was a freedom to be found from my sins and that the only way I could be rid of them was to cast all my care upon the Lord Jesus.

After a while the devil began to tempt me with doubting thoughts. I would wonder whether I truly was forgiven and I managed to persuade myself that this new-found freedom was not genuine but was just a nice feeling.

I went again to stay with my sister and, as usual, we went to Oxford chapel. Mr Morlan preached on the different signs of conversion. One he mentioned was doubt. This seemed kind of strange to me. In my inexperienced way, I assumed that all of God's children were confident of the fact they were saved. Mr Morlan explained that doubting thoughts are actually an attack from the devil. If you were not a child of grace then the devil would have no need to attack you but if you are, then the devil becomes worried and puts these thoughts into your head. This was a real encouragement to me.

It was during this period of doubt that we had Mr Andy Clarke come and preach at Westoning. I cannot remember much about what he said but I can remember the verse he preached from. The verse he preached from was:

'My sheep hear my voice, and I know them, and they follow me'.
John 10:27

March 2011

Not long after this time I was baptized at Westoning Chapel with my grandad Dawson (my dad's father, who has been a preacher for many years and was the retired Pastor of Westoning Chapel) and assisted by Mr Morlan. When I joined the church at Westoning, my grandad gave me the Bible text of 'Looking unto Jesus'. How little did I know how much my faith would be tested over the next few years.

Eight

Becca was pregnant. I was so excited. I couldn't wait to be an auntie again. As far as I was concerned being an auntie was the best feeling in the world. I couldn't wait to meet my new niece or nephew. Knowing my sister as well as I did, I had already guessed what they were going to call their baby. There is nothing quite like the excitement that new life brings to a family. Becca went for her first scan and it was during this that the first concerns were raised about the child Becca was carrying. As the pregnancy progressed the professionals began to inform Becca and Steve that everything was not as it should be. After more scans and consultant appointments they were told the devastating news that there was a strong possibility that the child would not survive until Becca was full term, and if the child was born it would not live long.

The days of Becca's pregnancy loomed in front of our family and each one that passed was an answer to prayer. It seemed that not a week went past without Becca having to go for some appointment or other. People far and wide all over the country were praying for the life that grew inside of her. Despite the fact that the professionals painted such a dark picture, we knew our heavenly Father is over all things and we took courage from this. I didn't allow the prospect of saying goodbye to my sister's child enter my head. I was sure the professionals had made a mistake and that God was going to prove them all wrong for His own glory. The faith of my sister and brother in law amazed me, as they were able to continue with the pregnancy despite the pressures placed on them by many people to put an end to it.

I went to stay with Becca and Steve again one weekend, while Steve was on call. We were on our way to chapel on the Sunday evening when Steve had a call. As we were all in one car Steve had to turn around and take us all home. We pulled back onto the motorway and hit stationary traffic making us all groan. It didn't make sense. There we all were sat in the car on a Sunday evening stuck unable to move. We began to wonder why, and I know I certainly questioned God's timing. What was the point of us being stuck here when we could have been in church and still have time for Steve to drop us home before he went out on call? When the traffic eventually moved we headed home and Steve went straight out. Becca and I settled Kezia down and I decided to keep Becca company for a while before I took the long drive home back to Bedford. We sat down on the sofa with a cup of tea and our conversation turned to their unborn child. I was still convinced that the professionals had it all wrong and everything was going to be fine. Becca spoke with confidence saying how the Lord knows what He is doing and no matter what happens all will be well. She was open about her fears and concerns, but I sensed a sense of calm and comfort coming from deep within her. I drove home praying like I had never prayed before.

The following day Becca called to say that she had written to Mr Morlan and she was going to be baptized. I was not surprised as I knew Becca had been a Christian for many years. A lot longer than I had. She was baptized on the 8th October 2011. It was such an amazing testimony to those who came along. Her public confession of faith at such a tough time was clear evidence of the grace of God in her life.

March 2012

Christmas came and went, with each day that passed, I felt sure to be confirmation that all will turn out well. March 31st dawned. The day after Kezia's birthday. The phone rang. It was Steve. Becca was in labour. The hours dragged by. Each minute that passed without news was more agonizing than the last. None of us could put our minds to anything. My brother Tom was home for the weekend so we all decided to go for a walk. It was a quiet walk. You could almost feel the prayers ascending from us as our feet fell along the familiar paths. Finally, after what felt like hours, we had a call. It was Steve. Daniel John Wigley had been born. Praise the Lord! He weighed exactly 10 pounds. What an amazing answer to prayer. That little boy was a true miracle. God had allowed him to be born into this world despite all the doubts that he would. We were all so excited, especially Mum.

Time could not pass quickly enough so we could go and meet him. Baby Daniel was transferred to a specialist hospital for further tests in the middle of his first night in this world. But Becca was discharged from hospital the next day. We went to visit Becca and Steve the day following little Daniel's birth and it was such a difficult path that they were walking. The joy of new life in their family was overshadowed by the distance between them and their son and the concerns about his health. It was a truly exhausting time for them both. After many tests and examinations Daniel was diagnosed with a heart condition. He remained in hospital for ten days following his birth and Steve and Becca regularly completed the 50 mile round trip to visit him taking Kezia along when they could so she could bond with her new baby brother. The day that Daniel came home was a truly special day. They went to pick him up and it's always amazing how the smallest member of the family always has the most stuff! The whole family was overjoyed to know that its youngest member was coming home. Home to the place where he belonged. God had answered thousands of prayers. The specialists had given the warning that Daniel would either grow out of his condition or die suddenly.

It was a real privilege to go and stay shortly after Daniel

came home. I felt overwhelmed with love as I watched Steve and Becca care for their precious child. Daniel had regular medication and they were so gentle and patient as they gave it to him. I was very aware of the tension that had been present over the last few months and was determined to give Kezia some special attention. The bed where I slept was in her room and as soon as she woke in the mornings she would stand up gripping onto the side of her cot, looking at me and trying to get my attention. Never being much of a morning person I struggled to wake up but was always pleased to see that dear little face smiling at me. I would sleepily get out of bed and lift her up and put her into my bed. Trying to get her to settle down I would snuggle her under my duvet. She would cuddle up sticking her well sucked thumb into her mouth. However, being just two years old and never one to stay still for long this lasted for all of ten seconds. She would then find different ways to amuse herself by poking me in the face until finally I would give her my sponge bag to rifle through. Together we explored the different products inside, having a little sniff and trying out the different potions on our legs and having a right old giggle. We all had many happy occasions with the little family. Each of us storing up treasures in our memories not knowing what the future held.

May 2012

May the 18th dawned.

It was a Friday. Over in Chinnor, Oxfordshire the Wigley family were stirring. Daniel was lying on his parents' bed, his legs kicking. Kezia was bumbling around playing between her own room and her parents. Steve was getting ready for work. Becca sat on the bed watching the proceedings. Daniel was smiling. His first smile. The little family crowded round to witness this milestone each trying to make it happen again. A while later Steve left for work and Becca set about getting the children ready. She was off shopping today. No small feat with a two-year-old and a new-born.

Over in Bedfordshire the Dawson household was also stirring. Dad was off to work, as was I and Mum was at home for the day. The work day was much like any other. I was glad it was Friday. This weekend I was planning to go and stay with Becca and Steve and I couldn't wait. About midmorning I was outside in the garden with the children. The phone in our room rang. My colleague answered. A minute later she came to the door.

"Deb, your mum's on the phone."

That's strange, I thought.

"Hello."

"Deb," came the panicked voice,

"Your dad's on his way home to pick me up. Daniel has stopped breathing. We are going straight to the hospital to meet Becca and Steve. Mr Morlan is on his way too. I've tried calling Tom but I can't get hold of him. Will you try?"

I assured Mum that I would and the conversation was soon over, with Mum promising to keep me updated.

My vision blurred. I grabbed hold of the unit in front of me, struggling to focus. Putting the phone back on its holder I stayed standing, staring at the wall for a moment. Mustering up the courage I turned around. The room was empty everyone was outside. Walking blindly, I headed for the door. I needed space. I needed to get out. Not sparing a thought for the ratio of staff to children in the room I headed straight to the toilet. Slamming the door behind me I lent my head against it trying to fight the sobs rising up inside me. Regaining control, I returned to the room. I managed to tell my colleagues what had happened and thankfully I was able to go on my lunch break. Grabbing my lunch out of the fridge I took my keys and went and sat in the car. I began to pray pleading that the Lord would perform an amazing miracle. When I had finished praying, I called Tom's mobile. It was off. Being a specialist optician in the NHS I was unsure of which hospital he was working at. Calling Cheltenham which I knew was his base I was told that he was over in Gloucester. After several more attempts I managed to speak to somebody who would pass a message on to him. This done, I looked at the time: my break was nearly over. The thought of eating my sandwiches turned my stomach. I sat prayerfully watching my phone willing it to ring. My lunch break over I began to get out the car when my phone rang. It was Mum.

"Daniel is with Jesus," was all she said before she put the phone down.

My heart broke.

Several hours later I walked up the path to Becca and Steve's home. Dad opened the door. Mum was on the floor playing with Kezia. I took one look at Mum and could see she was barely holding it together. Kezia seemed happy and contented. She spotted me and toddled over for a cuddle. Dad had encouraged Becca and Steve to go for a walk together so they could have a good cry. It wasn't until later they told me what had happened. Dad had been at work when he had received a call from Steve to say he was on his way to the hospital and could they come. Becca had been out shopping with both Kezia and Daniel in the pram. She had heard Daniel make a noise. Looking in at him she saw that he was beginning to turn blue. Spinning around she headed straight outside the shop. She got Daniel out of the buggy and laid him on the concrete floor outside the shop. Kezia remained in the buggy whilst Becca was on the phone to the ambulance service and started to try and get some breaths in him. Some passers-by, seeing what was happening, stopped and came over. The ambulance arrived very quickly as the ambulance station was only a mile away.

When they arrived, they scooped up Daniel and Becca was told there was only room for one and Kezia had to be left behind. Becca had to quickly decide and a stranger went in the ambulance to continue CPR whilst Becca, along with two further members of the public, followed. One of these worked at the local hospital and knew the quickest route and nearest place to dump the cars in the hospital grounds.

Becca was able to contact Steve, her husband, at work and he arrived at the hospital soon after them. As soon as he arrived the doctors and specialists announced there was nothing more they could do and Daniel had passed away.

Dad had frantically driven home to pick up Mum who was ready and waiting. They started out on their journey which took twice as long as normal. Every possible obstacle was in their way; road works, tractors, red lights, and diversions were all placed in their way to slow them down. It is beyond our knowledge as to why they were prevented from getting there sooner but we know that God is over all things.

When Steve and Becca came back from their walk, they both looked pale and drawn. I wanted to wrap my sister in a hug but knew she needed her space. What to say in a time like that? There truly are no words. I looked at two of the people who I loved the most in this world and wished there was something I could do to help. The one thing they wanted more than anything nobody could give them. We decided to get fish and chips for tea, despite none of us wanting to eat. We sat at the table, all of us trying our best, if not for ourselves but for little Kezia. She knew something was wrong and looked at the faces of her parents, her eyes asking questions her lips could not. Climbing up into her mum's lap she snuggled down. I watched Becca kiss the top of her head and a tear rolled down her cheek. I praised God for that little life.

In the times when tragedy strikes you suddenly feel as though your whole world has ground to a halt. There you are in your cube of grief and shock and you are looking out through the window of it at everybody else going about their business. Nobody stops to look at you. They are all happy and content with their own life. It feels strange to think that your world has suddenly become black while theirs is still sunny. Part of you feels like banging on the glass and shouting "Don't you realise what has just happened?" But then you stop and think. Why would they realise? You try to carry on living inside your cube but nothing can penetrate it. You wish you could open the door and run away leaving behind the tragedy and just melt into the crowd like everybody else. How much we take 'normal days' for granted.

The days and weeks that followed were incredibly testing. Steve and Becca began to plan Daniel's burial and memorial service. Adding to the stress, Steve began to have difficulties at work. The company decided to change their working patterns, meaning that he would have to work on Sundays. Things then took another turn for the worse. A few days before Daniel's funeral Grandad Dawson went into hospital to have a routine operation. All appeared to be well and he was sent home to recover. Several days later he was taken ill and admitted to hospital. It wasn't long before he was placed in intensive care the beginning of a long hospital stay during which time he was acutely ill fighting for his life. My dad, who had just lost a grandson, was now facing the prospect of losing his father.

The day of Daniel's burial dawned. Dad got up early and went to see Grandad in hospital. He was strong enough to say a few words and we knew he was sad not to be coming with us. We made our way to Chinnor. Arriving early, we sat in the car outside the little church where Daniel was to be buried. It was a beautiful sunny day. The sky was bright blue and everything seemed to be vibrant and full of life in the May sunshine. Becca had decided that she didn't want everybody to wear just black but had asked us to wear something blue in memory of Daniel. I sat there fingering the blue necklace I had chosen when I noticed in the mirror another car pull up behind us. It was the undertaker. Suddenly I felt sick. This was actually happening. The sunshine no longer looked beautiful. A little group of people were making their way up the path. Steve and Becca leading the way gripping tightly onto each other's hands with the Morlans following closely behind. I could not even begin to imagine the agony they must be going through. We got out the car to meet them. The undertakers were there at the gate, ready to greet the sorrowful little party. We walked together to the spot where Daniel was to be buried. There are no words to describe how it felt to see that tiny little coffin in the ground. We stood there, the Wigley family and the Dawson family united by the death of a precious child. Grief was etched on everyone's faces and I couldn't help but wonder why. Why had God allowed this tragedy to strike our family? I looked around at the faces of the people I loved and knew that by God's grace we would be able to persevere. I prayed earnestly that God would use Daniel's little life to be a blessing to many. As I sit here and write this I think, with amazement, what a testimony to God's grace Becca and Steve have been. When you look back you wonder how you have the strength to get through and there is only one way. God gives it to you.

Following the burial, we all made our way to Oxford chapel for Daniel's memorial service. Lots of friends and family were there which was very encouraging. Becca had also invited the people who had so kindly helped her on the day that Daniel passed away and it was lovely to see and meet them. Tom and I sat in the pew behind Becca and Steve. Mr Morlan did an excellent job of taking the service which can't have been an easy task. The hymns Becca and Steve chose were beautiful, one of which being 'When Peace Like a River' which is one of Becca's favourite hymns. Sometimes it takes a tragedy for people to really sing the words in hymns with their whole hearts. This is certainly the case with me. Glancing up I caught sight of Steve. He had tears pouring down his dear face. I swallowed and tried to get my own emotions under control. It was then that I noticed. He was singing. Singing his heart out. My heart broke and I let the tears spill onto my cheeks.

Deb with baby Daniel

On holiday in Thassos, (Greek Island)

Picnic at Bradbury Hill, blue bell woods

**On the phone to Mum while having chemotherapy at Oxford
and writing this book at the same time!**

Nine

June 2012

My grandfather was still incredibly ill and seemed to be getting progressively worse. Sometimes I stayed with Grandma at night to keep her company. On one such occasion we had both gone to bed and after much tossing and turning I had managed to get off to sleep. I woke to the sound of my phone ringing. It was Dad. My heart plummeted. This could only mean one thing. I quickly answered.

"Grandad has taken a turn for the worse, they might operate. Wake Grandma and tell her. We might need to go down there and see him before they take him to theatre. Wait for me to call."

I assured Dad that I would tell Grandma. He hung up.

I looked at the time: 2:30 a.m. I tentatively went and stood outside my grandparents' bedroom door. As I stood there, preparing to knock, I was suddenly taken back to my childhood.

I remembered standing here before, plucking up the courage to knock. My cousin Lella and I had been staying over in the summer holidays. We were sharing the room next door, she was fast asleep with a broken arm propped up on pillows, I had woken in the night and been sick over the side of the bed. I'd got out of bed to tell my grandparents, frightened of how they would respond. They thought I'd said I'd been sick in the bed and spent a long time searching through the covers looking for it. I remember standing watching them wondering what on earth they were doing! What a time my grandparents must have had dealing with us both! It made me smile.

I gave a gentle tap on the door and waited. There was no answer. I gave a harder tap and this time opened the door to peek inside. Grandma was beginning to stir so I went and sat on Grandad's side of the bed. There was no easy way of passing on the news, so I decided that best way was just to come out with it. I told her what Dad had told me and together we sat there waiting for him to call. It wasn't long before he did and as quickly as possible we got in the car and headed to the hospital. I had never driven so fast and on several occasions, I just told Grandma to shut her eyes and hold tight! She managed a small laugh and I was glad. All I wanted to do was get her there safely so she could see Grandad. None of us knew if he would ever make it through the operation. Pulling up at the hospital, I abandoned the car and took Grandma up to the third floor where Dad and Mum were waiting. Together Dad and Grandma went off to see Grandad and I went to move the car. We had made it in time.

Grandad's hospital stay seemed to drag on for ages. The discovery was made that when he had had his first operation the surgeon had made a mistake which had left Grandad incredibly ill. He was so bad that he was in the critical care unit on life support under sedation. Following his second lot of surgery, he began to improve and he was able to eat a little and hold a conversation for a short time. As the days and weeks progressed, Grandad was moved out of the critical care unit onto a normal ward where the real recovery was to start. We all began to relax a little and prayed in earnest that we would see Grandad preach again.

All the time that this was happening my thoughts and prayers were never far from Becca and Steve. They were fighting their own battles having the heart-breaking task of sorting Daniel's things and even finding the strength to get up each day. What a blessing little Kezia was to them at this time. It's strange when a tragedy of this kind strikes a family how the world seems to be full of constant reminders of what you have lost; whether it be an advert or a friend who has a baby, or even a shop window display, they all seem to be screaming out at you as constant reminders. The only way to survive these times is by continual prayer for that supernatural strength that can only be a gift from our heavenly Father.

Not long after Grandad began to improve Mum started to get pains in her stomach and side. We all dismissed them as indigestion or heartburn but it soon became apparent that it was something more severe. After a visit to A and E she ended up being kept in and we didn't know why. Days and days went by and still there were no answers as to why she was in so much pain. Dad and I struggled on at home with both of us having full time jobs and trying to fit in hospital visiting as well. Although we were tired, we were busy and sometimes being busy in these situations is the best thing. For Tom and Becca, it was a different story as they were both living some distance away and was a lot harder for them to come and visit.

It turned out that Mum had gallstones, so Mum was discharged and was put on a low-fat diet and a few weeks later the successful removal of her gallbladder was completed and Mum made a good recovery.

Ten

December 2012

Becca and I were getting ready for a trip to London. We had both been invited to go with a group of friends to the Royal Albert Hall for a Christmas concert. In true sisterly fashion we had decided to make a day of it and go out for dinner beforehand. We were up in Kezia's bedroom putting on our makeup. She was sat on the floor and I was kneeling in front of her applying eye shadow. It had gone unusually quiet in the room, Becca turned around so she could see what Kezia was up to. There she was also sat on the floor. In her lap was my sponge bag. She had managed to open a tube of body lotion and was calmly applying it to her leg using one finger blissfully unaware she was being observed. Becca looked at me, and I laughed.

"That's your influence," Becca said with a raised eye brow

I tried to look innocent but was secretly pleased. Again, I had been letting Kezia rummage through my sponge bag when I stayed. It was fun to watch her explore the different potions and smell them together!

When we were finally ready, we left Steve in charge of Kezia and rushed off to the next village to catch our train. Several months had gone by since Daniel's passing and I was pleased that Becca and I had decided to go. The last year had been incredibly painful and I really hoped we would both enjoy ourselves. As we parked up Becca checked her watch. If we were quick, we would be able to get the next train. We rushed to gather our bags and I quickly grabbed a pair of black shoes out of the car and put them on. I was wearing a new dress I had bought the week before on our annual Christmas shopping trip with our dad. It was bright red and felt lovely and elegant. We rushed down the road towards the station. I looked down at my feet and suddenly noticed that the shoes I was wearing were odd! They were both black but one had a small heel and the other was completely flat. I called to Becca and she turned.

"Look at my shoes!" I said, laughing.

She turned and walked a few steps and leaned over to look. Remaining bent over she began to laugh. It was as if we could both finally release our tension. We stood in the middle of the street laughing. The tears were streaming down our faces (so much for all the effort we had put into our makeup). Finally, our giggles subsided and we managed to regain our composure.

"I can't walk around London like this," I managed to gasp out.

"Is the other one in the car?" asked Becca.

"I don't know, let's go and check."

We returned to the car still rushing. I opened the car and there to my relief were both the missing shoes.

Once on the train we settled down to enjoy the journey. Our conversation centred around fixing me up with an eligible young man! Becca was keen to set me up and was happy to chat about the possibilities. I had been praying for what felt like years for God to provide me with a husband. The life I had previously lived still bothered me and I was aware that not many Christian boys would want anything to do with me. I felt as though everybody was still talking about me and speculating over what I had done. In truth, I was ashamed. Despite this, it was still fun to chat with Becca about what I hoped would be my future. We had a lovely time together wandering through the big department stores and enjoying a meal out.

We met up with the other people we were attending the concert with, outside the Royal Albert Hall. Introductions were made and I felt shy. Before finding our seats, we decided to go to the toilet. As usual we queued outside the ladies and it was at the point that I got talking to a young man. He was the brother of an old friend and part of our group called Matt. My memory of the conversation is dim. Let's just say we had a little disagreement about the appropriateness of a football game in the Royal Albert Hall. Little did I know many more similar conversations were to follow.

We found our seats in the hall and I ended up sat a few seats away from the chap I'd just been chatting to. The concert got underway and all attention was on the music happening before our eyes. I was captured by the live orchestra and felt myself begin to relax as the music washed over me. The interval came and people began to chat. Feeling shy again, I was glad when it was soon time for the concert to restart. The second half involved much more audience participation and I enjoyed singing along to the carols. Once the concert was over, we all filed out and congregated outside the hall. Becca and I knew if we were quick we could get the next train. We didn't linger over saying goodbye and left the group chatting outside. We began to head away from the Hall, for some reason, I turned to look back at the group of people huddled together. One was turned looking straight at me. It was Matt and for a moment our eyes met. It was as though we had said something without opening out mouths. I spun back around in pursuit of Becca, not giving the moment another thought.

It was New Year's Eve. Mum, Dad and I were staying with Tom in Cheltenham, where he lived and worked as a specialist optician. We were off to IKEA in Bristol so that Tom could buy a bed for his spare room. After much discussion, we decided to take two cars so that we were sure we could fit the bed in. Finally, we were all ready to leave and started to pile out of the door. My phone beeped. I paused to read the text. It was a message from Matt Cooper, the chap I met at the concert. He was wondering whether we could meet up some time. My face must have shown my shock because all the others turned to look at me.

"What is it?" somebody asked.

I slowly read out the text. The questions then began to

pour my way.

"Who is he? What's he like? Where did you meet him?"

I answered them as best I could until Mum burst out with "You never said anything!"

I tried to assure them that it was as much a surprise to me as them. The interrogation finally stopped and I got in the car with Dad while Mum went with Tom.

"What do I do, Dad?" I asked in desperation. My heart was heavy with the thought of having to tell my story and then face the rejection which I felt I deserved. "What Christian boy would ever want to marry a girl like me?"

I felt sure that he couldn't be aware of who I was. Matt is in fact Steve's cousin, so I thought it would be a good idea to text Becca to find out a bit more about him. She texted back almost instantly and I was able to find out a little more about him.

January 2013

The morning of our first date arrived. I was nervous. What should I wear? There were lots of clothes in my wardrobe but never quite the right thing. I settled on a denim skirt thinking it would look okay with my wellies. I went down stairs and showed my mum. She approved. That was good enough for me. We had arranged to meet in the car park in Woburn so we could go for a walk. It was only about a twenty-minute drive from our house. The whole way there I was praying so hard. Praying that the Lord's hand was in what we were doing and it wasn't just foolishness. The butterflies in my tummy grew more and more active the closer I got. I nervously kept half an eye on time. I didn't want to be too early and look too keen but I also didn't want to be too late because that was just rude.

Pulling into the car park I had a scout around. I couldn't see him. He had told me he drove a black Fiesta. 'How boring,' I thought. 'That's not a good start, driving a black Fiesta.' My opinion of people that drove Fiestas made them the least likely to be boyfriend material, despite the fact I drove one myself! 'I hope he's not some anorak,' I thought to myself, or this was going to be a very long day. If things were going really bad, I could always cut the walk short and call it a day. A black Fiesta sped into the car park. It was a new model. The Zetec S. Was it him? The car pulled in next to me. Hmm maybe things weren't going to be so bad. I suddenly felt sick.

'Well,' I said to myself, 'I can't sit here all day.'

I got out at the same time he did. He was tall with dark hair parted on one side with the rest swept over. He had a dark shadow of stubble which gave him a rugged and handsome look. Hmmm. Not bad looking! Not bad at all! I suddenly felt flustered when I realised he had been talking to me. Did my thoughts read on my face? I certainly hoped not. We agreed to go for a walk first and then to get coffee after. He undid his boot and pulled a pair of brown Timberland work boots. He sat down in his car to put them on. I couldn't believe it! I had a bit of a secret liking for men in work boots!

I couldn't tell you everything we talked about on that walk but I know that I soon felt free to talk and I was comfortable in his company. After our walk and coffee, we decided to head to a zoo which was not far away.

Several days had passed and I had still not heard from Mash. I had found out that Mash was Matt's childhood nickname and to me this suited him better, so Mash it was. In my mind I thought we had got on well but, as I told my parents if he wanted to see me again, he would have got in touch by now.

Mum said, "Why don't you just text him?"

"No," I replied, horrified, "it's up to the guy to make the first move."

"Hasn't he already done that?" said Dad in his usual dry way.

'Parents, what do they know!' I thought to myself as I headed outside to wash my car, leaving my phone inside glad to have a break from it. I came back inside to refill the bucket.

"Your phone went off," said Mum from behind the ironing board. Not wanting to appear too keen, I decided to fill the bucket before going to see who it was from. Probably just the phone network I thought to myself. Unlocking my phone, I eagerly scanned the screen, and there it was a text from Mash.

"Well?" said Mum.

"He wants to meet at Oxford on Saturday!"

I could almost see the relief go across Mum's face.

March 2013

Several dates later we decided that we wanted to carry on seeing each other and that it was time to tell people that we were going out.

I loved it when Mash called me his girlfriend, I felt so special. In fact, Mash certainly knew how to treat a girl. I had never in my life been treated the way he treated me. We managed to see each other most weekends and would spend them with family or off out exploring somewhere or other. Sometimes he would arrive with a massive bunch of flowers and at birthdays and Valentine's Day he would shower me with gifts. He loved to take me out to dinner and did lots of research into the best restaurants to go. We would talk for hours about nothing in particular and he never failed to make me laugh. I was reminded of something my Dad had said a few years earlier about me needing a man who would take me fine dining and treat me like a lady. Despite all of this outward display of affection, there was a deepness to Mash that I was discovering. To the rest of the world he was a rough and ready boy who enjoyed treating his girl. To me he showed a kindness and thoughtfulness I'd never seen before. I could also tell that he had two sisters, Karen and Sarah!

Summer 2014

As our relationship grew stronger, I began to wonder whether Mash had started to think about getting married.

The thought was never far from my mind but I was too shy to bring it up. It was the year of the World Cup and Mash, being a big football fan, was enjoying watching as many games as he could. I had decided to myself that I would wait for the World Cup to be over before I would broach the subject with him. One weekend he came to stay and on the Saturday, we decided to go and play tennis together. We headed to the local courts in town where we had such a laugh as I was absolutely hopeless and Mash spent the entire time chasing after the wildly aimed balls I had hit. After we had exhausted ourselves, we decided to walk to a local restaurant and get a drink. We sat outside chatting when a car pulled up in the car park and out of it got a bride and groom.

"Look at that!" I said. "That must feel amazing, imagine how good they must feel."

As soon as the words had left my mouth, I regretted them. I must have seemed so forward and what a massive hint! I waited tentatively for Mash's reply. To my surprise he agreed with me and thus began our first conversation about getting married. I was so excited. It felt like a massive answer to prayer. Mash told me that he had thought about it and even discussed it with his best mate Titch. We sat there talking about where we would live and where we would go to chapel. The hours past and neither of us took any notice.

The following day was Sunday and we went to chapel at Westoning. Mr Morlan was preaching and Becca and Steve, having moved from Oxfordshire to Bedfordshire in the past year, were entertaining him and his family at their home for the day. In the afternoon, we went around to see them all. It was tea time and we sat there enjoying Becca's lovely home made cakes. Suddenly the conversation took an unexpected turn, and before I knew what was happening, Mr Morlan was asking Mash when he was going to propose. I was so shocked. Poor Mash. I didn't dare look at him. Staring at the floor, I wished I could crawl underneath the sofa. I was thankful for the conversation we'd had the day before.

Eleven

July 2013

The summer continued and with it came a letter in the post. It was from the doctors. I had been called for my first smear test. I was scared at the thought of going so I ignored it. I cannot remember how many more letters they sent but eventually I came home from work one day to find my mum had booked the test for me. It was with great trepidation that I went for the appointment and like most of these things, they are never as bad as you think they are going to be. The nurse told me to expect the results in about a week and off I went, not giving it another thought. Several days later I came out of work to find a voicemail from the doctors asking me to ring them. Not thinking anything of it, I got in the car and headed home. Arriving home, I was greeted by mum who told me the doctors had called the house phone and left a message asking me to ring them back. She handed me the phone and I called them. The lady I needed to speak to had gone home and I was told to try again in the morning. Again, I didn't give it much thought.

Being on a late shift the following day meant I could call the doctors first thing in the morning. As soon as I told the receptionist my name, she seemed to know who I was and put me straight through to the nurse. I cannot remember exactly what she said but the gist of it was that my results had come back and they showed that I had cancerous cells on my cervix. This meant that I would need to go to hospital and have them lasered off. I came off the phone and felt like I was in a dream. Mum was looking at me and I knew I had to tell her but I just couldn't seem to find the right words. Even though the nurse hadn't used the word cancer it still felt as if that was what I had been told.

August 2013

The following week I went with Mum to Bedford Hospital
to have my laser treatment. It was a very uncomfortable
procedure that I would not wish to repeat. The doctor told
me that he hadn't managed to burn away all the cells and
that I would need to be put out for them to do so. An MRI
scan was ordered so they could have a look at the full extent
of the cells. Despite the seriousness of the situation, I still
thought in the back of my head that all would be well.
Again, Mum came with me to the scan and a few days later
I had a call to say that they wanted to see me with the results.
This time Dad came with me. We sat waiting for what felt
like hours in a waiting room full of pregnant ladies. Finally,
they called us into a room and we were followed by two or
three other people. It was a small room with a few soft
chairs and Dad and I sat next to each other on a small type
of sofa. To our left sat what must have been the consultant
and opposite us a nurse. The nurse was carrying several
leaflets and booklets which she put on a low table. I looked
at them and one word jumped out at me: Macmillan. She
caught the direction of my gaze and hurriedly picked them
up and hid them from view. It was too late. I knew I had
cancer. What followed was an explanation by the consultant
of what the situation was and what their plan of action was
to be. I remember Dad asking some questions and before
we knew it the meeting was over. We blindly stumbled our
way to the car and I had one phrase repeating over and over
in my mind that the consultant had said, "It's okay, you will
still be able to have children."

Somehow Dad managed to drive home.

The next day after this appointment was a big day. My
grandad Dawson, who had been so ill, was now eighty and
all of the extended family were together to celebrate. We
decided to keep the news of my diagnosis a secret from
everyone so as not to spoil the celebrations, that had been in
the planning for some time. With much help from the Lord,

we were able to put a brave face on it and get through the day. Unbeknown to me, in a quiet moment during the day, Mash asked my dad if he could marry me. What an amazing man, Mash is, the day after I had been given a terrible diagnosis, not knowing what the future held, Mash quietly asked my dad if I could be his wife.

About a week later I had an appointment at Addenbrooke's Hospital in Cambridge. The purpose of the visit was to put me out and have an internal look to determine exactly what sort of surgery I needed. Mum came with me and we sat together waiting anxiously for my name to be called. My consultant came and introduced himself to us. I didn't take much to him. When my name was called, I was taken into a room and told to lay on the bed. All around me people we bustling around. I was so cold in just my thin hospital gown. My whole body shook and no matter how hard I tried I couldn't stop it.

"Are you cold?" asked a friendly face. I nodded. She carefully laid a blanket on me and tucked it in. Shortly my consultant appeared, this time wearing scrubs.

"We need to ask you a series of questions."

Gradually all the staff gathered around me.

"Name?" he abruptly asked.

"Date of birth."

My voice was trembling as I stuttered out the answers.

"And finally, in your own words why are you here today?"

I looked around at all the faces staring at me. One at the end of the bed drew my attention, she was younger than the others. I looked at her badge. 'Student' it read.

"I'm here to see if I need a hysterectomy." I could hear my voice breaking. I looked back at the student and her eyes were filled with tears.

When I came round, I was being wheeled back to the bay where Mum was waiting. I was so pleased to see her. The nurse came with tea and toast and I began to feel much better.

Mum and I sat there in another of those situations that feels like you're in a dream and any minute you're going to wake up. It wasn't long before the curtain around our bay was pulled back and my consultant's face appeared. He looked at me lying on the bed and said very abruptly

"You're going to need a hysterectomy."

Before we could register what, he had said the curtain was back in place and he was gone. We turned to each other. Mum's face mirrored exactly my own feelings. We were in total shock.

August 2013

Mash asked me to be his wife! I was down staying with Mash and his family for a few days before we went on a summer holiday with my family. We went on a picnic together by the River Thames, I won't say much about what went on between us, except it involved me not having a clue, and some pesky swans that resulted in us having to move the picnic blanket several times! And yes, Mash did get down on one knee. I said YES! He gave me a beautiful diamond and platinum ring. I was so overwhelmed with joy and love for this amazing man.

Karen and Sarah made a beautiful engagement cake and we had a fun time celebrating with Mash's family.

The next day we were going on holiday to Wales, so we packed the car with a ton of stuff and Mash drove. Dad had kept it a secret when Mash asked for permission to marry me. Tom rang me on the way to Wales asking how our journey was going and I was bursting to tell him our news but we wanted to tell him in person. I think I was a bit off with him on the phone, because he later said to Mum, "Something is wrong with Deb, she's being really funny on the phone."

Little did they know the something, was something good for a change.

We all met up at the house we were staying in and Becca,

Steve and Kezia came to see us from where they were staying with their caravan. Mash and I were able to share our exciting news.

Dad just grinned; he thought it had been fun keeping such a lovely surprise from everyone.

We had a lovely and fun holiday; the house that we were staying in was very near the beach. We were able to spend days on the beach where Kezia loved 'surfing', playing in the water, and going off for secret ice cream stops with Dad! We were able to go into the sea, body boarding or hiring canoes, and then we would run up the beach in our wetsuits to use the showers at the holiday home and get changed to then return to the beach. It was an ideal location.

One night, after an evening meal at a local restaurant, Mash ever up for a spot of fun, suggested a night swim! Tom and Mash stripped off to their boxer shorts and ran into the sea, it was pitch black and cold. On the shore we couldn't see what was going on, all we could hear were gasps and moans of how cold it was. After a very quick swim, Tom and Mash ran out of the sea, they then had to walk through the town in just their boxer shorts back to where we were staying. We delighted in walking slowly to embarrass them and to ensure they were as cold as they could get!

How thankful we as a family were for this holiday, what a blessing it was, we all enjoyed it as much as we could, knowing I had my operation booked for when we returned home.

September 2013

I opened my eyes. All around me were bright lights. I was lying on my back on a bed. Somehow the bed was moving. Ahead of me some doors opened and I seemed to glide through. The walls were white and I could hear people talking. Was that Mash's voice? Hang on a second, someone was holding my hand. I looked to my right and saw my mum talking to a man wearing blue with a matching hat. It was then that it hit me. This was not a dream. This was reality. I had just had my hysterectomy. I closed my eyes again. When we stopped moving I opened my eyes to find I was on a ward. Mash was sat next to the bed and Mum and Dad were stood beside me. I tried to shuffle up the bed but incredible pain shot through my tummy. Something was on my face. I reached up to move it only to be told a firm "no" from Mash.

"What is it?" I asked.

"It's your oxygen." A nurse was busy explaining how I had a morphine pump and anytime I felt pain to push a button which would immediately administer the drug straight into my vein. I looked down at my hands they looked swollen.

"Mum, where's my ring?" I asked. Mum smiled and carefully got my engagement ring out of her bag. Mash gently pushed it onto my swollen finger. I wasn't sure what the time was and how long I had been in surgery. Somehow it felt like a long time. Mum must have been here all day.

"Mum, have you had your tea yet?" She wearily shook her head.

"You had better get some," I said, worried. I then thought about Dad and remembered he had been at work all day and now he was here.

"Dad, have you had your tea?"

"No." He smiled.

I was too tired to talk any more. Mum and Dad prepared to leave as it was getting late and I needed to rest. Mash was going to stay with me a bit longer. Before they left, Dad prayed. I can see him now standing there beside my bed his voice breaking as he committed us all to our Heavenly Father. At his amen I looked up and saw him wipe his eyes.

"Don't cry, Dad," I said "I'm gonna be okay"

I wanted to wrap my arms around the best dad in the world and take all his hurt away. Mash stayed with me when they had gone. I asked him about his day but he told me not to talk but to just rest. There he sat, gently holding my hand.

I drifted in and out of sleep aware of his presence and sometimes hearing his voice. How little did we know that this was to be the beginning of many other similar situations.

The next morning, I woke to find I felt terrible! I was in a lot of pain. The nurses were busy making sure everybody was getting up and washed. I lay there thinking, surely, they don't expect me to get up! How wrong I was.

"Have you had a wash yet?" asked a brisk nurse.

"No," I replied.

"Well if you get up, we can change your bed."

"I don't think I can do it by myself," I replied. She stood and watched as I sat up. The pain was so deep inside I thought I was going to pass out. I pressed the morphine pump and swung my legs round to the floor. Wheeling my drip in one hand and supporting me with the other, the nurse led me to the bathroom where I sank onto a chair placed in front of the sink. I looked up at my tired face and wanted to cry.

"I'll get you some towels," said the nurse and off she went.

I sat there exhausted by the effort of walking the short distance. The pain was so bad it felt as if my insides had been taken out stirred up and then put back in! I was terrified of looking at my tummy. Before the surgery had taken place, I had been told they normally manage to carry it out by keyhole, but on the odd occasion they would have to make a large cut. Somewhere in my anaesthetic memory I thought I'd heard somebody say that the keyhole wasn't working and I was going to have to be cut open. I was convinced that when I took my stylish hospital gown off I would see a big cut. Being a very squeamish person, I was terrified with how I would cope with such a thing. At the slightest hint of blood my head normally span and dots would appear before my eyes!

The nurse returned and wanted to know why I hadn't got started yet. She disappeared, saying she would be back soon to help me. I sat waiting and she didn't come. All I wanted to do was get back in bed. The time ticked by and I eventually realised she wasn't coming back. I was going to have to get on with it by myself. My hands shook as I gingerly lifted the front of my gown. I didn't dare look down. I tried to take it off but got tangled with the line in my hand. I needed help. Mustering what tiny little bit of courage I had I looked down at my tummy. There in a neat row were three tiny cuts. All this pain for those tiny cuts! I thought I would have more to show for it. Some people are never happy!

The surgery was carried out on the Thursday and on the Saturday, I was sent home. Everybody was so kind to me. Mash was there to take me home. He was so careful not to drive over any potholes or bumps in the road. The poor boy had a wincing fiancée in the front and a worried future mother-in-law in the back. I wasn't the only one who couldn't wait to go home. When we arrived home he and Mum helped me into bed and made sure I was comfortable. My bed had never felt so good. We shared some precious hours together as we chatted about our future. The following few days were difficult as I tried to get the balance right between resting and regaining my strength.

About a week after my surgery I began to feel unwell. Mum was the first to notice and was insistent that something wasn't right. As the day progressed, I began to feel increasingly worse. She tried phoning the doctors later on in the day but the phone just kept ringing and nobody picked up. Not being one to give up easily Mum put on her shoes and coat and marched straight out of our front door, down the street, across a road and into the doctor's reception. There she was greeted by two receptionists busy decorating a Christmas tree. No wonder nobody was answering the phone! It was not long before closing, but a doctor agreed to see me if I could get over to the surgery. Mum marched right back home bundled me into the car and we drove the thirty second journey to the surgery. After checking me over the doctor was worried that something wasn't right and suggested we go to A and E at Addenbrooke's. She called ahead to let them know we were coming. Dad drove at breakneck speed all the way. By this point I was really beginning to feel very unwell. When we arrived, Dad dropped us off and went to park the car. We were finally called and sent into a little side room where I was asked hundreds of questions. I tried as best I could to answer but I was in a lot of pain. The nurse seemed very incompetent and I was sure I had answered some questions twice. He even asked me if I was pregnant, even after I had told him my history. This made me want to hit him.

Even to this day I get asked that question. How much pain and heartache could have been prevented on many occasions if someone took the time to read my notes before asking me. Eventually I was put on a trolley bed. The department was extremely busy so I lay on the bed in the corridor waiting for something to happen. After a long wait someone came and took some blood and put a cannula in. Mum and Dad were worriedly waiting by the side of my bed. We were near the ambulance bay and it was busy with paramedics and hospital staff hurriedly passing through swinging doors. After several hours, I was taken into an assessment room where suspicions were raised that I had an infection. I was placed on a drip and began to feel somewhat better. After waiting several more hours, a bed became available for me on a ward and I was taken up. Mum and Dad followed to see where I was and then left to go home. It was about 2 a.m. and they had a terrible job finding the car which Dad had parked down a side street.

The following morning, I was assessed by the doctors as they did their rounds on the wards. The doctor wanted to have a closer look at me and asked me to wait in the consultation room across the corridor. He told me there was a possibility my bladder had been damaged during the surgery and they might have to re-operate. I made my way to the room and sat down on the bed and waited. The room had a window and I could see people passing. The nurses were busy going about their duties and other people passed by all walking with a sense of purpose. The minutes ticked by and I began to wonder if I had been forgotten. I carried on looking out the window but nobody seemed to notice me. My thoughts turned to the situation I was in and suddenly everything began to feel very bleak. I began to really think about the future and what it would mean not to be able to have children. It was the first time I had really allowed myself to consider what it might be like to never feel the joys of being a mother. A blackness engulfed me and I began to cry bitter, angry tears. As time went on my anger turned to sadness. I suddenly felt very alone. Even though the corridor was full of people I felt as though I had been abandoned. Not only by the medical staff but by my Heavenly Father. I was so alone. As I sat there a verse from the hymn 'How Firm a Foundation' suddenly came into my head. There I sat with my legs dangling over the side of the hospital bed, tear marks staining my cheeks, staring through the window like a prisoner. With a trembling voice I began to sing aloud,

"When through fiery trials thy pathway shall lie,
My grace, all-sufficient, shall be thy supply
The flame shall not hurt thee; I only design
Thy dross to consume, and thy gold to refine."

It suddenly dawned on me how foolish I had been. As a Christian I am never alone, no matter how bleak things may appear. I began to pray that all of my dross would be consumed and I would be made gold.

After several days of painful and undignified tests, I was allowed home having been diagnosed with a bad infection. The antibiotics I was given helped to clear it up and I began again what I thought was the road to recovery.

About a week later, I began to feel more unwell than usual. I emailed my consultant to let him know and he requested that I come into hospital for a check-up and blood tests. This time Becca took me. After having been checked over they could find nothing wrong and sent me home again. Becca took me back to their house where Mum and Dad were waiting. We hadn't been in through the door many minutes when my phone rang. It was the hospital, they wanted me back. My bloods results indicated that I had another infection. Dad took me home and we quickly packed a bag and set off for Cambridge A and E. This time we moved through the processes a little quicker than previously. After being taken into a side room for an examination, Dad and I were left alone in the room. Minutes turned into hours and still nobody came. Dad paced up and down the length of the small room pausing frequently to look out of the small windows. It became evident that we had been forgotten. Eventually, a male nurse entered the room. He seemed surprised to find us in there.

"What are you doing in here?" he asked.

"We've been told to wait," I replied. He looked as though we had done something wrong.

"You shouldn't be in here. You should be out in the bay with everybody else."

He led us out into an area with beds and bays in. We blindly followed, unsure of what we had done wrong. The same routine followed and after several more hours I was taken up onto a ward and it was time for Dad to leave. There is rarely a time when I haven't cried whenever I've been left in hospital. This time was no different. As I watched the figure of my father leave, he looked so forlorn. I just wanted to protect him.

Again, the hospital carried out lots of tests and scans to discover what was wrong with me. They found that after my lymph nodes had been removed in the operation my body was struggling to deal with the lymph fluids. My consultant informed me they might have use a needle to draw away some of the fluid. I was petrified. I hated needles. They would need to carry out another scan first to determine whether or not to go ahead with the procedure. I was beginning to build up a good rapport with my consultant, despite our rocky start. He laughed when I said I was scared.

"After everything you've been through, you can do this little thing. It's nothing!" he replied.

"Nothing! Having a needle stuck in your tummy is nothing?!"

"It will be alright," he said, smiling at my indignation.

I wasn't convinced.

Mum and Dad came to visit. They hadn't been there long when a porter arrived to take me to my scan. Dad decided to come with me while Mum waited up on the ward. They wheeled me down to the scanning department where we were left to wait in a sort of waiting area. It was a cold and stark room with several other patients on beds waiting too. We seemed to be waiting ages and as usual other people came and went but yet we remained. Dad didn't have a chair and just stood there by my bed. I felt so sorry for him. At long last it was my turn. I went into the scan knowing my dad was just outside the room praying for me. When it was all over we had to wait for a porter to take me back to the ward. The doors swung behind us as I was pushed through into the ward. They wheeled me past a waiting area and I could see Mum. She was smiling. She stood up and as she did someone else did too. Suddenly I recognized who it was. It was Mash! 'Hang on a minute,' I thought. 'What's he doing here? He should be at work!' He had driven all that way just to see me.

A few days later and I was home again. It was time to begin planning our wedding. There was so much to do and I was glad of the distraction. We were waiting for results to see whether I would need any further treatment. When they performed the surgery, they took samples from around the area where the cancer was and sent them away for analysis. It was hard waiting for the results. I was resting in bed one day when my mobile rang. It was my consultant.

The results had come back clear.

I was free of cancer!

It felt as though a huge weight had been lifted off my shoulders. I called for Mum and she came rushing. When I told her the news, she wrapped me in a hug and the tears flowed. I called Mash at work and he too was over the moon. God had not only answered our prayers but those too of all the people that had been praying for us. It felt as though we had been given a new start and a chance to begin again planning our lives except this time we were planning them together and it was so exciting. Despite the prospect of all that was to come, I was still struggling with the thought of never having children. I'm sure I went through a grieving process for the children that I was never going to have. It was to take months and years before I really came to terms with what had happened and even now it is still a struggle. One that is hard to admit. The grace of God is powerful and gives strength when there is incredible weakness. Without His help we are feeble and unable to continue.

Twelve

One benefit of being off work sick was that I had time to plan our wedding. The planning couldn't have come at a better time and really gave me a sense of purpose and lots of little manageable tasks I could take my time with. As I began to grow stronger, Mum suggested one day that we go and try on some wedding dresses down at the local bridal shop. We made an appointment and Becca came along too. We really didn't think we would find one but thought it would be a good place to start. Several hours later and two minutes before the shop was due to shut our purchase was made.

I was the owner of a beautiful wedding dress!

I could not wait to wear it again. Now began the hunt for bridesmaids dresses. I had decided on green as the colour as I knew it was Mash's favourite. We had lots of fun going around different shops, with Becca and I modelling lots of different styles. After visiting what felt like hundreds of shops we found some beautiful dresses that we thought would suit all of the bridesmaids. They were such special times. On one occasion, Kezia was with us and we had a good old singsong in the car. There we were travelling along, the sun shining, the love of our heavenly Father with us, and our hearts full of love as we sang at the top of our voices the familiar children's hymn about how with Christ in the vessel we can smile at the storm! I often think of that moment when things get hard, that with Christ by our side we can indeed smile at the storm with the grace that he gives us. It may not always be an outward physical smile but a deeper joy; knowing that we are safe and loved.

July 2015

The day before Deb and Mash's wedding was a day of torrential rain, one of those summer days that feels like winter; dark and very damp. Deb's mum was particularly concerned as the wedding reception was in a marquee. Deb, her mum, dad and Becca were carrying out errands. They squelched across the lawn to the marquee in the pouring rain trying to look on the bright side and trying not to get the stuff wet. Deb had worked so hard in the previous months making bunting, favours and handmade labels in the run up to her wedding, it would have been terrible to drop them in the mud! Each was praying that the weather would be improved by tomorrow.

The morning of the wedding arrived, everyone peeked out of their bedroom windows. It was a glorious summer day, not a cloud to be seen. It was a miracle, an answer to prayer, after the downpours the day before.

Mash and his best man Titch were sleeping on Steve and Becca's living room floor. They didn't get much sleep, as the excitement and apprehension built. The boys were rudely awakened at a ridiculous time in the morning, by a very excited bridesmaid, Kezia, jumping on their beds and requesting stories to be read by her uncle Mashy.

After Becca and Kezia were taken over to Deb's mum and dad's house to get 'beautified', as their dad would say. Mash's parents arrived to make sure the boys were behaving and were looking presentable.

In the Dawson household there was a flurry of activity with hairdressers, florists and commotion everywhere. Mash's sisters, Karen and Sarah, were also there helping with Kezia and getting ready to be bridesmaids alongside Kezia and Becca.

Amidst it all was Deb, a radiant bride. Her beautiful long curly, raven hair, which had required no attention from the hairdressers except to attach her veil. This was the day Deb had prayed about and dreamt about for many years. A day that had seemed impossible not only to her but also to her family. God had blessed her with an amazing man in Mash, a strong and dependable man. A man that loved Deb so very much. Deb turned and caught her brother's eye, and they shared a look and a tearful hug, no words were needed as a silent conversation ensued between lifelong friends.

The wedding party arrived at Westoning Church, the ushers (Tom and Steve) had done a good job in ensuring all the guests were firmly in the Church when Deb arrived. Then to the triumphant sound of Marion Copperwheat playing the Elizabethan Serenade, Deb walked down the aisle, on her dad's arm to meet her beloved. Mash turned and caught a glimpse of Deb. He wasn't fixed upon her stunning dress, or anyone else. It was Deb's beautiful eyes. Eyes that spoke volumes to him in one brilliant flash of love.

Deb's grandad, Mr Dawson, joined them in marriage. It was an emotional time and Mash's grandad, Mr Cornford, was able to give an address to the newly married couple. Mr Cornford spoke from a text in Jeremiah

'The Lord hath appeared of old unto me saying, Yea I have loved thee with and everlasting love: therefore with loving kindness have I drawn thee.'
Jeremiah 31:3

One of the hymns that they chose was Mash's favourite 'Will Your Anchor Hold'. How little they knew that in the coming days this hymn would be a testimony of their life together.

As Deb's grandad said quietly to Mash "You may now kiss your bride," Mash gently lifted Deb's veil, and kissed his bride. There was hardly a dry eye in the church.

A delightful reception followed, with friends and family enjoying the sunshine, sharing and rejoicing in Deb and Mash's day. There was even some last minute 'gate crashers' who turned up to witness the special day. So many people loved Deb and Mash, and wanted to be with them as they celebrated their marriage. Speeches were given and everyone commented on the delicious slow cooked lamb.

It must have been a very nervous day for Tom's new girlfriend Felicity, meeting lots of family and friends for the first time. But Tom looked so happy as he stood and introduced the glamorous young lady, it truly was, such a joy to behold.

The day ended in Mash and Deb driving away in Deb's Fiesta, with the clanging of cans, balloons popping, and toilet rolls billowing out behind them

It can be put in no better words than what Deb said "It was the best day of my life".

Late July 2015

Off on honeymoon we went. We spent the first couple of nights in a posh hotel in Oxford, so we could spend the Sunday at Mr Morlan's church. This would be our home church, as we had bought a house in Bourton near Swindon. We enjoyed surprising Mr Morlan and the church family who knew we had just got married. We then travelled on to Cornwall for the rest of our honeymoon. Mash in his usual romantic way had planned and arranged it all as a complete surprise. Our honeymoon will forever remain between Mash and I. A truly treasured time.

A few symptoms started to show themselves and I thought they were nothing, but Mash said, "You really ought to get checked."

I really didn't want to. So not long after our honeymoon, we took a trip back to Addenbrooke's Hospital to see my consultant. After scans and lots of different things, it turned out that the cancer had come back.

But this time it was even worse. It was attached to different places and touching different organs.

It was at this point I was transferred from Addenbrooke's Hospital to be under Swindon and Oxford, as we lived closer to these hospitals.

I had some more major surgery, then I went through some intensive treatment, I had six weeks of chemotherapy and radiotherapy.

The treatment was very intense.

We lived near Swindon and all the treatment was in Oxford and I had to be there for 8 o'clock in the morning.

Travelling to Oxford from Swindon was not the best journey. It was really tiring; my body was being attacked with all this treatment and it was a really testing time for us. I really struggled. I struggled with my pride. I was just married, I'd got a new life, I'd started my dream job and there I was, I couldn't even do my own ironing. I found it really hard because, again, I felt like my dreams were just being taken away.

I remember one time Becca came to stay. She hadn't been through the door about five minutes and I started haemorrhaging all over the floor, all up the stairs everywhere. It was so scary. So again, I was back into hospital. It was a really difficult time.

After my surgery, chemotherapy and gruelling daily trips to have radiotherapy, I spent a week in hospital in Watford having brachytherapy. Not only was I away from home in a strange hospital the treatment was so painful. It was agony. I had to lie on my back perfectly still for almost a week. If I'd have known how painful it was, I don't think I would have gone through with it. Mash was able to visit me, driving down each day after he had done a day's work. My family were also able to visit and some kind friends.

There was one Sunday when I didn't feel well enough to go church so I listened to an online sermon. The minister was speaking about Elijah and how he had to wait by the brook and how strange it must have seemed. It felt like God was talking to me. I felt like I was wasting time. What good was I? I felt good for nothing and again I just prayed that I would be refined into gold.

My cancer was particularly bad and the consultant wasn't sure whether the treatment would work. I thought a lot about dying and as a Christian you kind of think, 'well when the time comes I will be okay' but it's actually quite scary to think about. I think as a Christian it's okay to acknowledge that you are frightened. Even the Lord Jesus Christ when He was in the garden of Gethsemane, He prayed 'let this cup pass from me' and that's how I felt, I didn't want to die.

February 2016

At the end of my treatment, I had what they call a PET scan. They put a radioactive substance in your body and anything that's cancerous will show up.

The results came back. They were all clear.

It was amazing. It was like I could start my life again. They said they would keep scanning me which they did regularly.

It felt like we could begin our lives again.

So, we began again, and started planning for the future.

Thirteen

June 30th 2016

June the thirtieth is Dad's birthday. It was the day we had a phone call to say the results were back from a recent scan I had had earlier in June. The voice on the phone asked, could we go in and discuss it with them. So, in Mash and I went with great trepidation.

There is no easy way to say this but the cancer had come back again and this time it had spread to my liver. I knew once cancer gets into your liver there is not really much that can be done. The professionals gave me one to two years to live. I remember praying on the way back that God would use my testimony for His glory and promised that I would use every opportunity to speak of His goodness to me.

We made the trip to Bedfordshire to tell Mum, Dad, Steve and Becca my recent scan results. What a birthday present, that was the worst part having to tell your family. You feel so helpless.

Again, I began treatment, more chemotherapy. It began to work, to shrink things, which was amazing. What was really difficult about this time, as in previous times I hadn't lost my hair, but this time I would.

August 2016

Mum and Dad had organised a surprise holiday. Mum had always wanted to pay for us all as a family to go away together on holiday. We were all told the dates to book off, and nearer the time were told a postcode to drive to and a time to meet.

We all met at the requested rendezvous point in Devon, in a Tesco's car park. It was so exciting. I think Mum was the most excited as she had been planning this holiday for over a year!

Added to the excitement, Tom and Felicity had just got engaged, so we were all offering our congratulations on their engagement in the middle of the Tesco car park, which was the meeting point. Here we were given three separate envelopes with clues in to the final destination, with strict instructions not to open them until we had finished the food shop.

So, into Tesco's we marched. I think it's safe to say there has never been a food shop like it, in the history of Tesco's and probably never will be. Three trolleys later, with Kezia getting underfoot, we blocked aisles as we held major discussions on what delicacies we needed, and how much food we might need as we must not run out! Going through the checkout was an embarrassment. I sat on the side-lines, watching and letting Kezia play with my phone. Becca embarrassingly decided it was her job to be the expedition photographer. She continued to annoy other shoppers by getting in their way whilst she was snapping away. Let's just say the food bill will remain a family secret between us children for a very long time!

After following Mum and Dad's clues, we found the lovely house where we were to spend the week. It was set in the Devon countryside on a farm. Mum had created bespoke signs for all our bedroom doors. Kezia's was a picture of a puppy like the one the family had just bought.

We settled into the holiday and on the Sunday morning we went to a place of worship quite far away.

Sunday afternoon we all did our separate things. Mash and I went off to have a sleep as the chemo was very tiring. Mum and Dad decided to go and visit the farmer's cows that were in a shed. It was then that Mum slipped going down a slope and with her wellies on managed to twist her ankle.

Dad and Mash took Mum off to the local cottage hospital, where they thought she had a badly sprained ankle. It was only later on that Dad got a phone call to say that they now thought there was a small fracture, and to go back on Monday.

It had been previously decided that we would spend the

evening worshipping together at the holiday home with Dad bringing a message from God's Word himself. So, with Mum's foot propped up, crutches nearby, Dad spoke on Psalm 103:13:

'Like as a father pitieth his children, so the LORD
pitieth them that fear him.'
Psalm 103:13

It was a precious family time together, with a message spoken from the heart.

On Monday Dad took Mum to hospital where it was confirmed that she had a fracture of her ankle. Mum returned with her ankle in plaster. Now this plaster was a sight to behold. It was absolutely huge, so white and big! Poor Mum, she had been planning this family holiday for over a year and to then break her ankle on the second day into it was such a disappointment. Not knowing how Mum was going to be we all cautiously enquired how she was. Mum just burst out laughing, seeing the funny side of it all.

"It's only my ankle," she said. We all joined in the laughter.

What followed was a few more hospital visits where thankfully they removed the plaster and provided a boot thing, which was much better. Mum was great and tried to not let it stop her doing anything.

If anyone has ever negotiated the beach with crutches and a very large plaster cast, you will know the problem it presents. So, in the usual way our family pulled together, we managed to get Mum on and off the beach by the men carrying her in a very large and cumbersome beach chair. It really was a funny sight; Mum semi-reclined, shrieking out "Be careful, don't hurt yourselves," white foot straight up in the air, the men puffing and sweating profusely, struggling up the beach. With us girls following, not sure whether to dissolve in giggles or try and hide in embarrassment at the amazed looks and comments of the other beach-goers!

We did have a lovely holiday sharing good times. We spent simple times around the camp fire, with me snuggling up to Mash. Sharing precious times together as a family. One evening Dad had arranged a private chef to come and cook a three-course meal. It was a truly amazing experience; one we shall never forget. The evening ended in Mash and I trying to teach everyone our newly learnt dances that we picked up on a recent holiday in Greece. It was a laughter-filled evening. Truly a time to remember.

We as a family were so thankful for this precious time together, although it was bitter sweet, knowing that I was terminally ill, and I had more gruelling treatments ahead of me.

As the holiday drew to a close I noticed that my hair was falling out; not just a little as you would sometimes expect but in handfuls. I guess the chemo was doing its job and the side effects were beginning to take its toll.

September 2016

I sat in front of our floor length mirror to do my hair before work. Picking up my wide-tooth comb, I ran it through the mop of brown curls. It stopped at a tangle and I gave it a firmer tug. Breaking free I pulled it away from my head and to my surprise a big clump of hair came with it. I stared at it not knowing what to do. Pulling it off the comb I had another go and the same thing happened. I kept repeating the process, strangely addicted to watching the lengths of hair break away from my head. I was collecting a pile of hair on the carpet. Looking down at the brown pile I stopped and the tears began to roll down my cheeks. I gasped and put my hand over my mouth. Bending double, the sobs began to come and my whole body shook. I gulped for air and looked up at my red blotchy face in the mirror. Reaching up I touched what was left of my hair and frowned at how tender my scalp felt. I thought of the Bible verse saying that every hair on your head is numbered. It felt like God was mocking me. Picking up the hair I held it in my fist and raised it to the ceiling.

My hand trembled as I shook my fist and shouted, "Well I hope you're keeping count now!"

The tears continued to roll down my cheeks and I felt bitter and sad. I pushed the bitterness away and thought of God's goodness to us. I knew the only way I could get through this was with the Lord's help and I was too weak to stand on my own. There was no way I was going to let myself be consumed with anger. I knew I could either revel in self-pity and bitterness or get on with the day.

I breathed a quick prayer of "Lord help me" and standing I went to my jewellery rack and pulled off a flowery scarf. Returning to the mirror, I had a go at tying it in a pretty bow. I managed to secure it and decided it didn't look too bad. The patches where the hair was missing were covered at least. Continuing to get dressed I began to feel the scarf gradually sliding off my head. The bitterness and anger began to rise up inside me again. I stomped around our bedroom muttering to myself. Returning, again to the mirror I assessed the situation. The hairline at the sides of my head was gradually growing bigger and next to my tan it looked very white. Almost laughable. Picking up the scarf, I decided to have another stab at it. Maybe some pretty earrings would help. I was determined to make this chemo thing an opportunity for a bit of glamour. The second attempt was a bit more successful. I sighed. It was time to leave. I was late as usual.

It was 5:30 p.m. and I had just arrived home. I slammed the car door shut and walked up the path to our house. I was feeling nervous about the scarf on my head. What would Mash think of it? Would he laugh? I knew in my heart he wouldn't but I still felt a sense of embarrassment. I opened the front door and cautiously put my bag down. I could hear him out in the garden so I walked through the house. Before he even had chance to say hello I burst out

"I know it looks silly but I needed to cover up my hair."

"I know," he replied, walking towards me.

I walked to meet him and he opened his arms to me. Snuggling into his chest I felt safe.

"It looks nice," he said.

I wasn't sure if he was just trying to make me feel better or not but I didn't care, I just loved the feeling of being home.

Several hours later, we readied ourselves for bed and I climbed in next to him. He snuggled up to me put his arm around me. I shifted to get more comfortable my hair caught under his head. Mash moved his head and a load of my hair came with him. He calmly picked up the strands of hair and put them onto the floor. The tears began to sting my eyes and I tried to hide them. Mash got back into bed and this time climbed on top of me. I turned my face into the pillow and tried to wriggle out from under him. There was nowhere I could hide and I couldn't fight it any longer. I let the tears seep out the corner of my eyes and before I knew it great big rivers ran their way down the sides of my face and landed in my ears!

Mash didn't say anything but gently wiped the tears away with one hand while scooping me closer to him with the other. I buried my head against his chest and let the flood gates of emotions open. When I calmed a little, he propped himself up on one arm and looked down at me. He gently ran his hand through my hair and looked into my eyes.

"You know you're beautiful," he said.

I shook my head, the tears threatening to start again. I certainly didn't feel beautiful and felt sure not many people would find me attractive.

"You are," he continued, "you always will be, whether you've got hair or not."

I looked into the eyes of my best friend and husband and gave him a small smile. I wanted to tell him how much I loved him but I knew as soon as I spoke I would choke up. I tried to hide my face against him but he gently pushed me down onto the bed.

"You are beautiful on the outside and inside in many

ways. You are the most beautiful girl I've ever seen."

This time I pulled him towards me, feeling comforted. I kissed his lips and settled back down thinking he would settle beside me. Instead he stayed where he was and carried on stroking my face. His eyes looked sad and I waited for him to say something. He just looked at me his eyes, speaking volumes.

"God loves me more than you do," I said.

Mash smiled, "and I love you an awful lot."

"He loves you more than I do," I continued.

He smiled and nodded and I reached up to stroke his face.

Beauty.

Fourteen

May 2017

I had a bad feeling about this appointment. The results from the last scan showed that the cancer was stable but unlike previous occasions it had begun to stop shrinking. Today was the day where we received the next set of results. If all was well, I was due to go straight from the consultant appointment into the day therapy unit where I would receive the chemo. As usual we went through the process of going for bloods and then the long wait in the two different waiting rooms. They called me in to weigh me and we knew then that it wouldn't be long. Finally, my name was called and we entered the consulting room. I am always thankful when medical professionals get straight to the point, and this time my consultant did.

She hit us with the news that the cancer in my liver had stopped responding to the treatment and had indeed grown. Despite being half prepared for this news, I still felt as though I had just been hit by a bus. My mind began to cloud and I struggled to concentrate. I was able to focus enough as she showed us two different scan pictures showing the changes. It was the first time I had actually seen my cancer on the screen, and for a minute I was fascinated. I found myself asking questions about what exactly we were looking at. In her usual fashion, my consultant did her best to answer but her responses were so vague that I felt there was almost no point in asking. I was keen to know how long she thought I would have left but she was unable to answer.

The treatment I had been receiving was going to stop there and then and there was no other alternative, apart from an extremely toxic dose of chemo that would make me very ill.

We were going to be referred to the clinical trials team

in Oxford but without any certainty that they would be able to help. The appointment ended and we made our way out. We walked past the entrance to the day therapy centre, and for the first time in my life, I wished I was having chemo.

The next day Mash's alarm was going off. I rolled over to see him reach out and stop it. 'Must have had some sleep,' I thought to myself as I knew I had just been woken up. Mash got up and I reached to look at my phone. 6:10 a.m. There was a message.

'Am coming to see you tomorrow morning if that's okay Love Becca'.

I looked at the time the message was sent. 10:30 p.m. the night before. I lay back down. My head felt as though it had been filled with cotton wool. So stuffy and full. I shut my eyes for a minute wishing I didn't have to face the day. I just wanted to stay right where I was and go back to sleep. At least when I was asleep I could escape from the nightmare that was happening for real. I wished that the appointment yesterday had been a bad dream and I had just woken up from it.

Once Mash left for work, I dragged myself out of bed. I felt sick. Knowing Becca, I knew she would soon be here. I managed to get myself dressed and it wasn't long before she arrived. Twenty-seven years of friendship gave us the liberty to say what we were really feeling. There was no need to pretend and I made no effort to disguise my feelings. We cried together and even managed to laugh. What special times.

Mid-May 2017

My consultant had told us there was a possibility I would be eligible for a clinical trial. We began to pray that one would come up and before long we received a letter asking us to come to the Oxford Churchill Hospital. Mash arranged time off and we found ourselves sat in a waiting room, in a hospital where I had received so much treatment and really hoped I would never have to visit again. We felt positive about the appointment and waited with great anticipation.

I was called in to be weighed and then finally the consultant was ready to see us. Like most of these appointments, we seem to spend the first few minutes wishing the doctor would get to the point and cut the small talk. He told us lots of information about taking part in a clinical trial and what some of the trials involved. It soon became evident that there were no trials available to me at that time. He reminded us of the alternative option of the very strong chemo and in my mind, this was not an option. My hair was beginning to grow back. I couldn't bear the thought of losing it again. How vain was I. We were sent on our way with the promise of a phone call in a few weeks' time to see how I was doing, and to update us on any available trials.

Mid-June 2017

Several weeks passed and no phone call came. Eventually a letter dropped on the door mat with an appointment with my consultant in Swindon. Having been suffering increased pain in my right side I thought it would be sensible for me to have a scan prior to the appointment. Calling my first point of contact, my Macmillan nurse, I received no reply as usual. After leaving a message and waiting several days, I began to get frustrated so resorted to emailing her. She replied the same day telling me that it would not be possible for me to have a scan. I was so angry!

At our previous appointment my consultant had told us that the threshold for me to have scans was low. I was so keen to know how the cancer was progressing, so that we could began making plans and have more of an idea of time scales. The day of the appointment approached and I began to rehearse in my head what I was going to say about not having a scan. I was convinced that I was being denied the scan due to NHS lack of money. If this was the case, we were prepared to pay for one ourselves.

Mash again organised time off work and we found ourselves travelling along the beautiful back road to Swindon hospital; a road we had travelled many times before having heard both good and bad news and in various different states of health.

Upon arriving at the hospital, we checked in at the desk only to be told that we had arrived early and my appointment wasn't for several hours. You can imagine what this did to my already fraught nerves. Knowing that we had arrived at the time requested in the letter I was furious and demanded that we were seen at the time we had been given. After waiting a while, we were told that it wasn't possible and to basically 'go away and come back later', which was exactly what we did.

Several hours later, we were finally seated in front of my consultant. Before I even had chance to open my mouth she began to explain that there had been some confusion and she had never said that I couldn't have a scan.

I was so surprised.

It was as though she knew exactly what I was thinking. It dawned on me that I had been carrying this burden around and worrying when all the while my Heavenly Father had everything under control. I felt an immense guilt when I realised that this was something that I hadn't even prayed about, but felt sure that somebody had on our behalf. During the consultation we were asked if we had heard any news regarding clinical trials. We replied that we had not, which my consultant thought was strange. She explained how she had referred me to the clinical trials centre at the University College London Hospital (UCLH) and I should have heard back by now. We were sent away with the instruction to get in touch if we had not heard anything by early next week.

The weekend passed and several days went by and still we had not heard. I emailed my clinical nurse specialist as instructed. Again, I did not hear back so decided to take matters into my own hands and do some chasing myself.

Weeks had gone by since the referral had been sent and I was at the end of my tether.

It took several days of chasing different people with numerous phone calls, when I finally discovered that the referral had never gone through. Several days, emails and phone calls later, the clinical trials centre was able to confirm they had received my referral. Now the waiting game began again. However, we did not have to wait long. The very same day I had a call from the centre requesting me to come down to London the following week and discuss with the doctor a clinical trial that was available to me. I was so excited and quickly called Mash so he could book the time off work.

July 2017

The following week we headed off to London. Having not travelled to London very frequently this felt like an ordeal in itself. If I was to be accepted onto the trial, this would be a journey I would be making regularly. After much discussion we decided to drive to Reading and catch the train from there. Not being part of the main hospital, we found the clinical trial centre sandwiched between two buildings along a busy street. It didn't look at all like a medical establishment and we wondered for a moment if we were at the correct place. Double checking the paperwork, it confirmed that we were.

With great trepidation we entered the building through the modern glass doors and found ourselves in a reception area monitored by a security guard. Opposite the entrance were a set of lifts, so we followed the instructions on the paperwork and selected the fourth floor. The next room we found ourselves in appeared to be a sort of waiting room. The receptionist took my name and we settled ourselves by the window enjoying the view of the busy street below. Having been to so many appointments we knew a long wait was to be expected. After what must have been an hour, the receptionist made a phone call telling somebody that

Deborah Cooper was still waiting. When he came off the phone he told us they weren't ready for us yet and did we want a cup of tea. This was not the sort of treatment we were used to!

Finally, sometime later a doctor called us through and we followed her through a security locked door into a corridor behind. She led us into a consulting room and we sat down, as so many times before, on the two chairs positioned for that purpose.

I was brimming with questions and hurriedly got my written list out of my bag. She wanted a full history and as succinctly as I could I told her about the last few years. Writing quickly, she paused now and then to ask a question. When she had enough information, she began to inform us about the trial we had travelled so far to hear about. We were able to ask our questions and things seemed very positive.

The next stage (if all concerned were happy) was to sign the paper work giving my consent to take part in the trial and acknowledging my understanding of all that was involved. One of the requirements for being put on the trial drug, was a biopsy of the active cancer. In order to carry this out a scan was required and so we were sent away with assurance that I would be needed back in London soon for a scan and blood tests.

The scan date came and this time Becca came with me.

A few days later the hospital got in touch to organise a day for my biopsy. The date was confirmed and my stomach began to churn with the worry of it all!

Fifteen

Mid-July 2017

The day of the biopsy approached and I had been feeling more unwell than normal. I was experiencing a lot of high temperatures and a general feeling of being unwell. I was still plodding along at work but everything seemed more of an effort than normal.

Having done some research, I put the temperatures down to the type of cancer and tried not to worry. When the date had nearly arrived, I decided to ring the hospital just to let them know about my temperatures, in case I got all the way there only to find they wouldn't do it.

The specialist nurse sounded very concerned and recommended that I got straight to A and E. I came off the phone feeling very annoyed. I didn't have time to be unwell, and I knew if I went down A and E there would be little chance I would be coming home.

Mash was at work, so I called his sister Sarah who had her day off to see if she wouldn't mind taking me. I told her not rush and an hour or so later she arrived. I called Mash to let him know what was going on. He told me not to pack a bag as he was sure I wouldn't need to stay in and if I did he would bring one later.

We didn't wait long in the waiting room before they called us through. The first thing they did was to take my temperature. It was high.

Sarah looked surprised.

"You need to take your coat off," the nurse said.

It was the last thing I wanted to do.

"And your jumper," she said.

Now that's just cruel I thought as I sat there shivering. After some more poking and prodding, we were allowed to go and wait in a bay.

"Will I be going home today?" I asked the nurse.

She shook her head, "Sorry but no."

I wanted to cry. Sarah and I made our way to the bay where there was no bed and were told to wait for one. Finally, one was ready and with Sarah's help I changed and got in. I felt terrible. But at the same time, I felt a sense of relief. For so long I'd been trying to feel well and had been telling myself that it was all in my head that when someone actually confirmed I was ill, I felt as if I could rest and let them sort me out.

My hospital stay lasted two weeks. There are so many things I could tell you about it and like most people who either work in or have stayed in a hospital, you could write a book!

This was a particularly dark time for me.

Our second wedding anniversary came and went and I was still in. Our much-anticipated holiday with my family also came and went and yet I was still in.

After spending some time in an acute assessment ward, a bed became available on another ward. A fine example of being thrown out of the frying pan and into the fire.

My new home was a ward full of old ladies with dementia. My heart broke at the different behaviours I was observing, and it did nothing to boost my morale. Sometimes I didn't know whether to laugh or cry.

A very sweet lady with advanced dementia would often come and talk to me and help herself to the food and drink my family had brought in! Sleep was often very scarce with some patients shouting out in the night or attempting to leave the ward.

One particular memory stands out in my head. The lady in the bed next to me had a really bad skin problem on her legs. Sometimes the nurses would come along and put cream on them as they were very dry and flaky. One morning I woke up to find all over the floor between her bed and mine, was what looked exactly like flaky pastry. The floor was absolutely covered, right up to the edge of my bed.

I was confused. Maybe she'd had a croissant for breakfast. Either that or a whole pack! As I lay there thinking about it, it suddenly dawned on me. That wasn't pastry. It was the skin off her legs. I suddenly began to feel a bit nauseous. Then angry. Why hadn't anybody had the decency to clean it up? Surely that wasn't healthy for infection control. I gingerly got out of my bed, the other side and picked my way across to the bathroom, all the while trying not to think about it. Thankfully the cleaners were always very punctual and I knew they would soon arrive. A few hours later, my lunch arrived. It was a flaky pastry slice!

My patience was wearing very thin as none of the doctors seemed able to give any answers as to why I was still in hospital. They had tried to find the source of an infection but couldn't. I had received every type of antibiotic they had available but to no avail. The only medication I was receiving was paracetamol and even when I had a peak in temperature and was desperate for it, I sometimes had to wait over an hour before I received it.

I wanted to go home.

One day a straight-talking oncologist came to see me to discuss a scan I'd had. He informed me that the cancer had grown considerably. I tried to find out about time scales from him but, like a typical doctor come politician, he found a way of answering and avoiding the question at the same time. I was no better off. Finally, in my frustration I asked him if I would live to see Christmas. His reply knocked me back.

"If the cancer continues growing at the rate it is then, no."

I didn't know what to say. I was glad he was frank with me but it wasn't what I wanted to hear. I couldn't wait for him to leave me alone. As soon as he was gone, I pulled the curtain around my bed curled up in a ball and cried. Christmas was only five months away.

August 2017

After a very long two weeks I was finally allowed home. Mum took time off work and came to stay to help me recover. I had to work on trying to eat properly and build my strength ready for the trial in London. It was touch and go whether or not I could get onto the trial.

The delay caused by my hospital stay meant that all of the tests and scans had to be redone. Several more trips to London and several more weeks later we were given the date for a liver biopsy with the hope of having treatment the day after next. Previous to the procedure, I had been reassured that the biopsy would be taken under general anaesthetic. However, when we arrived things had changed. I would be awake for the procedure.

That was it. I went into meltdown mode.

Much to Mash's embarrassment, I refused to have the procedure done unless they put me out. After some persuasion from a doctor and Mash, I agreed to have it done despite being awake. I was so petrified that when they were part way through the procedure they told me I had to stop shaking otherwise there was a possibility they could puncture a lung. With the help of my Heavenly Father I was brought safely through the procedure. They kept me in overnight to monitor me and Mash went off to the hotel he had booked which turned out to be a right dive.

He hardly slept.

In the morning, Mash awoke to a breakfast of baked beans and tomatoes – not quite the full English that was advertised – in a grubby dining room filled with grubby people. Whilst I was told on the other hand not to eat, but to drink a litre of vile liquid before a CT scan. Neither of us was impressed.

31st August 2017

Finally, the day for treatment dawned, and with great anticipation we made our way to the trial centre. After much difficultly with the canula we finally got underway. It was a long day but as we left the centre and got into a taxi I felt such a sense of relief and thankfulness.

September 2017

With the kind help of family who accompanied me to London every couple of weeks, I was able to continue with the treatment. The days were very long and the journey extremely tiring for all involved. The feeling of arriving home, seeing Mash, and getting ready for bed was something I dreamed about all day.

Sometimes the visits would be quite traumatic as the nurses fought to get cannulas in my already tired and worn out veins. My tolerance levels began to drop and I soon began to dread cannulation and blood tests.

The requirements of the trial were very strict and sometimes I would arrive for treatment and they would take bottles and bottles of blood and other times only a few. Despite this, in a strange sort of way, I looked forward to treatment days where I could spend a day with a family member which is something that doesn't happen very often.

Mid-October 2017

My first scan came and went with mixed results.

The agreement was to continue the treatment as I seemed to be coping with it.

And so, with God's strength, we continued our expensive train journeys and interesting taxi rides! We had some laughs!

Mid-December 2017

The time came for the next scan. As always, I lay there on the bed as I went into the machine fervently praying. Waiting for scan results is something you never get used to. Sometimes you got given a date for when your scan results would be ready. The day arrived and as usual we spent it in great suspense waiting for the phone call. Having not heard anything by lunchtime, I decided to give them a call. After being diverted several times, then told to call back again later I finally spoke to somebody who told me that not all of the results were back yet and she could tell me no more. I asked to speak to the doctor but as usual he was in a meeting.

My frustration grew as it felt like I had spent the last few years fighting for treatment and results. I had learnt not to believe everything I was told as things changed so regularly and facts altered overnight.

Anyway, to cut a long story short, late in the afternoon/evening I finally had a phone call from a doctor. It was then that I wished he hadn't called. I had long ago learnt what you don't know can't hurt you.

He had the unenviable job of telling us they were going to stop the treatment due to my latest scan results. The scan showed that some parts of the cancer had grown and other parts were now stable.

I was so confused.

Why stop it when there was clear evidence the treatment was doing some good? I tried to reason with the doctor but I soon learnt that the decision was out of his hands and that because of the strict criteria of the trial I was no longer eligible.

I came off the phone so angry. It took me several weeks to feel at peace about the news. I was so bitter. I couldn't understand how morally they could stop the treatment.

A few days after this news I had a call from the trial centre in London asking me go down for a blood test. I couldn't help but laugh on the phone. They must be joking! If they thought I was going to waste a day travelling all the way to London, on gruesome public transport for a blood test they had another thing coming! I soon told them what I thought of that idea. Finally, we managed to reach a compromise and I had the test done locally.

It felt a bit like we had been abandoned. I was now taking several drugs prescribed for me by London and they were closely monitoring me for any changes needed in dose etc. Who was going to take over? Again, I spent several days on the phone trying to arrange appointments to make sure that somebody was going to pick up the reins. It felt as though I was doing somebody else's job for them but knew if I didn't get on and do it then nobody would.

December 2017

It was nice not to have our lives interrupted by treatment again. With only a few weeks until Christmas, it was great to have something to look forward to.

Early in December, Dad made a round trip of four hours in the car to bring a real Christmas tree to us. We had saved our tree from a couple of years ago, and kept it in the garden. Admittedly it was a little small and a bit bare but we thought it would do.

Dad did not agree. He turned up one Saturday with a massive bright green real tree. It was huge, but beautiful. Dad spent the day with us and tears came to my eyes as Dad left to drive the two-hour journey home. What an amazing Dad, such love.

Christmas came and went and we had such a special time spent with both families.

So many memories to be treasured. Having been told I was not going to live to see Christmas it was very surreal and I just wanted to treasure each moment. Mash had been saying for a while he wasn't sure if I would like what he had bought me. I teased him saying it would be okay as long as it wasn't a dishcloth as I have a strong dislike of using them! Christmas Day arrived. After unwrapping our presents there was one box left under the tree.

"Here come the dishcloths," I teased. How wrong I was. Inside the box, packed in lots of packaging, was another small box. I carefully opened the lid and there inside was the most beautiful eternity ring. Words failed me and I just sat there staring at it in disbelief. Mash encouraged me to try it on.

There on the inside of the band were inscribed the words 'God will take care of you'. The tears began to roll down my cheeks. What a special man God had given me, one that I truly did not deserve.

Epilogue

Deb's writing finishes with her last entry describing the beautiful Christmas gift that Mash had given her.

The Christmas of 2017 was truly special. Christmas Day and Boxing Day was spent with Mash's family. A lovely couple of days attending church exchanging presents, dozing by the fire with memories to cherish.

Deb and Mash then went on holiday with Deb's family to stay in a hotel in the New Forest, that Deb's dad had arranged and paid for. It was such a precious and fun time together. Going away at Christmas was something Deb's family had always talked about. The family managed to take over any lounge they sat in, other patrons would poke their heads in the doors see the commotion and beat a hasty retreat, as presents were exchanged and lively conversations ensued.

The hotel even put the family in a separate area away from other guests for their evening meals. As the family glammed up each night, especially Tom in his evening jacket and the men in braces, different games were played in between courses, causing great hilarity. One example is a mission impossible demonstration, which involved Steve and a pair of braces. This will remain a funny memory with Deb's infectious giggle sounding out.

The family made a trip to the sea side and enjoyed beautiful weather in the New Forest, watching the ponies and racing remote controlled cars. Each evening and morning started off in someone's room with a time of prayer and reading God's word. The Dawson family had such a happy time together, not knowing if they would have another.

Another memory in Deb's last days is the time Tom asked Deb if it would be okay if he went on another of his mission trips to Africa. At this time Deb was in the midst of one her treatments and she selflessly replied "of course". She was always thinking of others and she wanted everyone to carry on living their lives, despite being very ill herself.

In January 2018 Mash was able to take as much time off work as he needed to spend time with Deb and take her to any appointments, and to look after her.

Mash's family went on a family holiday in early 2018 to Sussex, again spending family time together, and visiting Mash's extended family. In Deb's last few months she often felt sick, very tired and in tremendous pain, but she wanted to create as many memories as possible, doing as much as she could.

Deb had been praying for many years for Mash to make a profession of his faith and be baptised. As Deb's life drew to a close, she prayed fervently that she would see him baptised. On February 24th 2018, Deb's prayer was answered. Mash was able to stand before the church and congregation at Oxford and give an account of the Lord's work in his life, and be baptised. Although Deb was too weak to stand for the singing of the hymns and she even found singing difficult, she was able to praise the Lord and she was so thankful that her prayer had been answered.

It is very difficult to describe what Deb and Mash went through in Deb's last months. Mash's love and care for Deb was truly amazing as he patiently cared and loved Deb through the most difficult days of her life. Family and friends visited and spent precious times with Deb and quite often no words were needed.

Deb rarely thought of herself and as her pain increased and became agonizing, her only thought was for Mash and her family and how they would all be once she was in Glory.

One time Deb sat with her mum, quietly holding her hand and she said to her mum,

"I've wasted so much time when I ran away, please

forgive me, and Mum, please don't be bitter when I'm gone."

Of course, Deb's mum had forgiven her many years ago. Deb's mum recently recalled when Deb returned home, after running away, a lot of her clothes were missing and she didn't have a winter coat. Deb's grandad Baker gave her some money to buy a new coat saying that it was to 'be the best robe'. Like in the parable that Jesus told of the prodigal son returning home and giving him the best robe.

Deb and Mash's families believed that Deb spent many hours praying for Mash and them all, asking the Lord to help them after she had been taken home to glory. Many times, after Deb had passed away the families could almost feel the prayers of Deb being answered from the grave.

There is so much more that can be said about Deb's life, of the joy and happiness she brought to so many people. Also, it would be wrong not to mention the help and care Deb and Mash and their families received from so many people. Many, many people all over the world prayed and supported them through difficult times and still do. Deb and Mash truly proved that when you walk through the fire the Lord is with you and it is only through His strength and grace that you are able to continue.

'When thou passest through the waters, I will be with thee; and through the rivers, they shall not overflow thee: when thou walkest through the fire, thou shalt not be burned; neither shall the flame kindle upon thee.'
Isaiah 43:2

Deb's parents visited Deb and Mash the weekend before Deb was taken very ill. The following Monday, Deb was taken by ambulance to hospital in agonizing pain and from there to a hospice in Swindon.

One memory that sticks in the family's mind, on visiting Deb in the hospital, Mash's tremendous care and love. When Deb needed to visit the bathroom, it was the last time the family saw Deb on her feet. The picture of Mash so carefully and tenderly virtually lifting and supporting Deb's poor weak body with such love and care.

As Deb's life drew to a close, she never complained about her pain or circumstances. She looked with a certain and sure hope of her eternal home; she knew she was saved from all her sins, and God had forgiven her.

Deb loved Mash so very much, and he truly was the man of her dreams, that she used to dream about. He was her rock and support, a true blessing from the Lord.

When Deb lay nearing the end of her life in the hospice, she was almost unrecognizable.

Mash commented "she is still beautiful."

And she was still that beautiful girl.

One of the last things that Deb was able to say, was to her dad as he read some of her favourite passages from the Bible, which included John 14:1-6. It speaks of the Lord Jesus going to prepare a place for you in heaven and the mansions that await those who believe on Him.

Deb whispered "Nearly there."

And so, on that beautiful sunny morning of the 5th of April 2018 with Mash and her family present, Deb quietly drew her last breath. The angels came and took her home. There would be no more tears for Deb, no more sighing, no more struggle, no more pain. Deb wasn't 'nearly there', she was there, there in the presence of her precious Saviour, for all eternity.

'And God shall wipe away all tears from their eyes; and there shall be no more death, neither sorrow, nor crying, neither shall there be any more pain: for the former things are passed away.'
Revelation 21:4

Extras

PRECIOUS

The death of Daniel came as a big shock, even though we had been told by the hospital he could die at any time. He passed away on the 18th May 2012. I had a phone call from Becca while at work to come over so I went home to get Mary my wife, then straight on to Stoke Mandeville hospital. We kept on getting behind slow vehicles and one of the roads was closed so we had to take a diversion. We then had a phone call from Steve to say that Daniel 'had gone'. We were met at the hospital by Mr Morlan who took us to Becca and Steve, we went in to see Daniel for the last time, utterly heart breaking. All that is left is *precious* memories like seeing Becca hold him in hospital with some wires running from Daniel to some machinery. Taking him for his first walk through the bluebells in the woods with Becca and Steve and joking with them about all the clobber they were having to take. Watching Becca or Steve give Daniel his medicine, holding him and looking into his mischievous yet intelligent eyes. Daniel would be the very picture of contentment regardless of what was going on around him.

Our moments spent with Daniel were very *precious,* but we know he was more *precious* to our Lord. (Ps 139:14-18) As he was in the womb he was not hid from the Lord; he saw all Daniel's substance the Lord's thoughts towards him were *precious*.

'How *precious* also are thy thoughts unto me, O God!
how great is the sum of them!'
Psalm 139:17

Daniel was redeemed by the *precious* blood of Christ (1 Pet 1:18-19) the events around his death, even though very harrowing was under the eye of God. For we know that Daniel's death was also *precious* to the Lord for we read:

'*Precious* in the sight of the Lord is the death of his saints.'
Psalm 116:15

On Sunday 20th we all spent the day with Becca and Steve. We took our own picnic, then on the Monday Dad went in for a routine hernia operation I took my mum in to see him. On the Tuesday, Mary and I went over to Becca and Steve's and did some shopping at High Wycombe to get some clothes for Becca and Steve, for Daniel's funeral. We also looked after Kezia, while Becca and Steve went and registered Daniel's death and took some of Daniel's clothes to the undertakers for him to be buried in. We then had a look at the plot for Daniel's grave and had a meeting with Steve's parents and Mr and Mrs Morlan about the funeral.

On Wednesday 23rd Dad had to go into A and E. I went to work, then picked up Mum to go and see Dad in the critical care unit.

So, on the Thursday 24th I tried to get ready for my prayer at the grave side and my reading at Daniel's thanksgiving service. I took Mum to see Dad in the 12–2.00 visiting slot.

About 4.45 I had a phone call from hospital and spoke to the surgeon/doctor. He went into great detail about four times so I could understand. Dad needed an urgent operation, he may have a popped ulcer or a hole in his bowel it would be a very risky operation because of Dad's condition, he had gone in to multiple organ failure. Dad then spoke to me and asked me for my thoughts on what the surgeon/doctor had to say and also for my blessing/permission to go ahead with the operation.

We rushed down to the hospital with Mum, to see Dad before he went in for the operation and we saw the surgeon/doctor and the anaesthetist. They were very blunt about it all; only two out of ten survive. Spent some time with Dad before the operation. It was very upsetting and emotional. Called my siblings to come over. Stayed until the operation was finished, Dad was on a respirator and other stuff. Mr Morlan was with us until Dad went in for the operation.

Friday 24th, went into see Dad early in the morning, he gave us a wave then later we made our way to Chinnor for the committal. Becca and Steve coped very well, then we all went over to Oxford for the thanksgiving service this was taken by Mr Morlan who has been so good all along. On the Saturday morning I went with Tom to see Dad he just held my hand. I do believe that Daniel is with the LORD which is far better and that he was **'taken away from the evil to come' Isaiah 57 :1.**

But why has all this happened? 1 Peter 1:7 tells us **'that the trial of your faith, being much more *precious* than of gold',** may God give us the grace to see and feel this in all things.

'But our God is in the heavens: He hath done whatsoever He hath pleased.'
Psalm 115:3

This was written by Deb's dad, on the death of his grandson Daniel and when Deb's grandad Dawson was very ill in hospital. Deb's grandad made a very good recovery and resumed preaching, which the Lord has richly blessed to many.

It was Deb's wish that this was to be added to the back of her book.

Go in Peace

The following is an email that Deb's dad wrote to Deb, before she was going to give her testimony. Deb was concerned about giving her testimony and the motives behind people coming to hear her speak. Again, it was Deb's request that this was to be added to the back of her book.

Hi

Hope the attached is not too boring.

Shalom
Dad

'And when the messengers of John were departed, he began to speak unto the people concerning John, What went ye out into the wilderness for to see? A reed shaken with the wind? But what went ye out for to see? A man clothed in soft raiment? Behold, they which are gorgeously apparelled, and live delicately, are in kings' courts. But what went ye out for to see? A prophet? Yea, I say unto you, and much more than a prophet. This is he, of whom it is written, Behold, I send my messenger before thy face, which shall prepare thy way before thee.'
Luke 7:24-27

What went ye out for to see? Jesus knew the motives of those who went to see John the Baptist and went on to defend him:

'For I say unto you, Among those that are born of women there is not a greater prophet than John the Baptist: but he that is least in the kingdom of God is greater than he.'

So, when you go to speak you are not responsible for the
motives of those who come to hear you but Jesus sees them
and will defend you.

**'And all the people that heard him, and the publicans,
justified God, being baptized with the baptism of John.
But the Pharisees and lawyers rejected the counsel of God
against themselves, being not baptized of him. And the
Lord said, Whereunto then shall I liken the men of this
generation? and to what are they like? They are like unto
children sitting in the marketplace, and calling one to
another, and saying, We have piped unto you, and ye have
not danced; we have mourned to you, and ye have not
wept. For John the Baptist came neither eating bread nor
drinking wine; and ye say, He hath a devil. The Son of
man is come eating and drinking; and ye say, Behold a
gluttonous man, and a winebibber, a friend of publicans
and sinners! But wisdom is justified of all her children.'
Luke 7:29-35**

John was a sinner but Jesus stood up for him, now we see
this Pharisee inviting Jesus for something to eat:

**'And one of the Pharisees desired him that he would
eat with him. And he went into the Pharisee's house,
and sat down to meat.'
Luke 7:36**

But the meal was gatecrashed:

**'And, behold, a woman in the city, which was a sinner,
when she knew that Jesus sat at meat in the Pharisee's
house, brought an alabaster box of ointment, And stood at
his feet behind him weeping, and began to wash his feet
with tears, and did wipe them with the hairs of her head,
and kissed his feet, and anointed them with the ointment.'**

Luke 7:37

Jesus knew and so do we what the Pharisee was thinking:

'Now when the Pharisee which had bidden him saw it, he spake within himself, saying, This man, if he were a prophet, would have known who and what manner of woman this is that toucheth him: for she is a sinner.'
Luke 7:39

Again, Jesus is defending one of his people:

'And Jesus answering said unto him, Simon, I have somewhat to say unto thee. And he saith, Master, say on. There was a certain creditor which had two debtors: the one owed five hundred pence, and the other fifty. And when they had nothing to pay, he frankly forgave them both. Tell me therefore, which of them will love him most? Simon answered and said, I suppose that he, to whom he forgave most. And he said unto him, Thou hast rightly judged.'
Luke 7:40-43

Jesus clearly knows all about Simon and this woman:

'And he turned to the woman, and said unto Simon, Seest thou this woman? I entered into thine house, thou gavest me no water for my feet: but she hath washed my feet with tears, and wiped them with the hairs of her head. Thou gavest me no kiss: but this woman since the time I came in hath not ceased to kiss my feet. My head with oil thou didst not anoint: but this woman hath anointed my feet with ointment. Wherefore I say unto thee, her sins, which are many, are forgiven; for she loved much: but to whom little is forgiven, the same loveth little. And he said unto her, Thy sins are forgiven. And they that sat at meat with him began to say within themselves, Who is this that forgiveth sins also?'

Luke 7:44-49

Jesus knew that the invite to the meal was not genuine and to this woman it may have looked very posh and showy, but her motive was out of love to her Saviour and this is all that matters:

'And he said to the woman, Thy faith hath saved thee; <u>go in peace.</u>'
Luke 7:50

Guess the lesson is that you need not be too concerned about the reasons why people ask you to speak and the motives they have when coming to hear you.

Just do it for God's glory which I know you do. It is very hard to speak in public because you have to walk it out as well as speaking about it. The devil doesn't like it and will do his best to give speakers a rough ride.

Deb's response in a text to her dad was

Thank you, Dad. Just read your email.
It made me feel so much more at peace.
It wasn't boring at all.
I love you loads.
I hope you get on well today Xxxx

Lightning Source UK Ltd.
Milton Keynes UK
UKHW020356250321
380914UK00001B/13